The Complete UK Diabetic Cookbook for Beginners

2000-Days

Delicious, Low-Sugar & Low-Carb Recipes for Type 2 Diabetes, Pre-Diabetes and Newly Diagnosed, Incl. 4-Week Meal Plan

(Colour Edition)

Evenor Sherry

Copyright © 2024 By
Eve Ahmed All rights reserved.

No part of this book may be reproduced, transmitted,
or distributed in any form or by any means
without permission in writing from
the publisher except in the case of brief quotations embodied
in critical articles or reviews.

Legal & Disclaimer

The content and information in this book is
consistent and truthful,
and it has been provided for informational,
educational and business purposes only.

The illustrations in the book are from the
website shutterstock.com,
depositphoto.com and freepik.
com and have been authorized.

The content and information contained
in this book has been compiled from reliable sources,
which are accurate based on the knowledge,
belief, expertise and information of the Author.
The author cannot be held liable
for any omissions and/or errors.

Table Of Content

Introduction 1

Chapter 1: Navigating the Diabetic Diet 3

    Key Components of a Diabetic Diet 3

    Building a Balanced Plate 4

    Managing Special Diabetic Considerations 5

    Monitoring and Adjusting 6

    Lifestyle Factors and the Diabetic Diet 7

    Practical Tips 8

Chapter 2: Breakfast 9

    Protein Spinach Waffles 9

    French Asparagus and Courgette Omelette 9

    Homemade Cinnamon Rolls 10

    Apples and Walnuts Porridge 11

    Spicy Shakshuka 11

    Cheese Spinach Omelette 12

    Baked Eggs with Zoodles 12

    Egg and Mushroom Wild Rice Casserole 13

    Coconut Quinoa Breakfast Porridge 13

    Savoury Turkey Patties 13

Chapter 3: Grain and Rice 14

- Wild Rice with Parsley 14
- Mint and Pea Risotto 14
- Couscous with Balsamic Dressing 15
- Mushroom Spelt Bowl 15
- Nut Buckwheat Pilaf 16
- Apple and Pecan Quinoa Salad 16
- Spelt and Cherry Salad 17
- Pearl Barley with Peppers 17
- Quinoa with Spinach 17
- Blueberry Wild Rice 17

Chapter 4: Noodles and Pasta 18

- Turkey Spaghetti 18
- Chicken Fettuccine Alfredo 18
- Minced Beef Pasta 19
- Caper and Olive Pasta 19
- Spinach and Mushroom Pasta 20
- Cherry Tomato Farfalle with Pesto 20
- Creamy Tomato Pasta with Spinach 21
- Basil Tomato Pasta 21
- Penne Pasta with Tomato-Vodka Sauce 22
- Sesame Noodle and Courgette Bowl 22

Chapter 5: Bean and Legumes 23

- Herbed Black Beans 23
- Chickpeas Curry 23
- Rosemary White Beans with Onion 24
- Green Lentil and Carrot Stew 24
- Mexican Black Bean and Chicken Soup 25
- Lentils with Spinach 25
- Black Bean and Tomato Soup with Lime Yoghurt 26
- Easy Three-Bean Medley 26
- Black-Eyed Beans with Collard 27
- Adzuki Bean and Celery Soup 27

Chapter 6: Fish and Seafood 28
Cod with Asparagus 28
Spicy Prawns 28
Chinese Style Cod 29
Thai Fish Curry 29
Simple Salmon 30
Cod Cakes 30
Breaded Flounder 31
Sesame Seeds Coated Haddock 31
Thyme-Sesame Crusted Halibut 31
Tuna Salad with Lettuce 31

Chapter 7: Vegetables 32
Perfect Roasted Brussels Sprouts 32
Sautéed Cabbage 32
Low-Carb Cauliflower Mash 33
Vegetarian Caramelised Onions 33
Breaded Artichoke Hearts 34
Roasted Cauliflower with Lemon Zest 34
Asian Fried Aubergine 35
Ratatouille with Herbs 35
Cauliflower Mushroom Risotto 36
Grilled Ultimate Portobello Burger 36

Chapter 8: Poultry 37
Chicken and Spinach Stew 37
Barbecue Chicken Wings 37
Chicken and Mushroom Casserole 38
Herbed Turkey Breast 38
Whole Chicken Roast 39
Turkey Hoisin Burgers 39
Chicken Fajita Bowls 40
Broccoli Chicken with Black Beans 40
Easy Asian Turkey Meatballs 41
Chicken Curry 41

Chapter 9: Meats 42
    Air Fried Ribeye Steak 42
    Braising Steak with Brussels Sprouts 42
    Garlicky Lamb Chops 43
    Lamb Rack with Pesto Sauce 43
    Slow Cooked Lamb Shanks 44
    Garlic Pork Chops 44
    Crumbed Golden Fillet Steak 45
    Crock Pot Carnitas 45
    Nut Crusted Rack of Lamb 46
    Cajun Smothered Pork Chops 46

Chapter 10: Salads 47
    Quick Chopped Caprese Salad 47
    Avocado Cucumber Feta Salad 47
    Classic Carrot Apple Salad 48
    Caprese Salad Quinoa Bowl 48
    Lemon Avocado Tuna Salad 49
    Chickpea Salad with Olives and Cucumber 49
    Asparagus Salad 50
    Cherry Tomato and Avocado Salad 50
    Tuscan Tuna and Bean Salad 50
    Roasted Beetroot and Pistachio Salad 50

Chapter 11: Soup and Stew 51
    Calamari Stew 51
    Carrot and Bean Chilli 51
    Spinach and Beef Stew 52
    Tomato and Bean Stew 52
    Delicious Roasted Beetroot Soup 53
    Beef Tomato Stew 53
    Creamy Vegetable Soup 54
    Tomato Chicken Soup 54
    Mushroom and Beef Chilli 55
    Quick Lentil Bisque 55

Chapter 12: Starter and Sides 56

    Artichoke-Spinach Dip 56

    Red Peppers and Anchovy Antipasto 56

    Baba Ghanoush 57

    Tzatziki Greek Yoghurt Dip 57

    Healthy Grilled Asparagus 58

    Air Fried Olives 58

    Simple Grilled Prawn 59

    Classic Bruschetta 59

    Grilled Aubergine and Courgette with Balsamic Vinegar 60

    Spicy Sun Dried Tomato Hummus 60

Chapter 13: Snack and Dessert 61

    Cajun Courgette Chips 61

    Carrot Cupcakes 61

    Rosemary Baked Cashews 62

    Spicy Kale Chips 62

    Cream Cheese Pound Cake 63

    Spicy Chicken Bites 63

    Herbed Pitta Chips 64

    Cauliflower Tots 64

    Blackberry Crostata 65

    Cinnamon Bread Pudding 65

Appendix 1: Measurement Conversion Chart 66

Appendix 2: 4-Week Meal Plan 67

Appendix 3: Recipes Index 68

Introduction

Greetings, fellow food enthusiasts and diabetes warriors! I'm delighted to welcome you to "The Complete UK Diabetic Cookbook for Beginners," a collection born out of my personal journey with diabetes and the realization that many individuals in the UK face similar challenges. As someone who has navigated the labyrinth of diabetic living, I understand the struggles of maintaining a balanced and satisfying diet while managing blood sugar levels.

Living with diabetes often requires a reimagining of our relationship with food – a journey that I embarked upon with curiosity and determination. Through trial, error, and a passion for culinary exploration, I've discovered that maintaining a healthy lifestyle doesn't mean sacrificing taste. In fact, it's an opportunity to embrace a world of vibrant and wholesome flavours that not only nourish the body but also bring joy to the dining table.

In this cookbook, I present to you a carefully curated collection of recipes that go beyond the mundane constraints associated with diabetes. This book is more than just a compilation of dishes; it's a celebration of the rich tapestry of ingredients and the culinary possibilities that can thrive within a diabetic-friendly framework.

Inside these pages, you'll find a diverse array of recipes that cater to different tastes, preferences, and dietary needs. From hearty breakfasts to soul-satisfying dinners, each dish is thoughtfully crafted to strike the perfect balance between nutrition and indulgence. But this book is more than just a list of ingredients and instructions; it's a companion on your journey towards a healthier and more flavourful life.

I've also included valuable tips, nutritional insights, and practical advice on meal planning to empower you in making informed choices about your diet. With this cookbook, my aim is to transform the way you perceive diabetic-friendly meals – from a restrictive necessity to a delightful opportunity for creative and delicious cooking.

So, whether you're managing diabetes yourself or supporting a loved one on this journey, join me in embracing "The Complete UK Diabetic Cookbook for Beginners." Let's embark on a culinary adventure that not only nurtures our bodies but also tantalizes our taste buds. Here's to a delicious and healthful life!

Chapter 1: Navigating the Diabetic Diet

Diabetes, a prevalent metabolic disorder, significantly influences dietary decisions, playing a pivotal role in managing the condition. This introduction sheds light on the fundamentals of diabetes, its diverse types, and the intricate relationship between the condition and dietary selections.

Diabetes is a chronic medical condition characterized by elevated blood sugar levels, resulting from the body's inability to produce or effectively use insulin. As we delve into the dietary aspects, it becomes apparent that the impact of diabetes extends beyond mere glucose control-it significantly shapes what and how individuals consume.

Different types of diabetes necessitate distinct dietary approaches. Type 1 diabetes, typically diagnosed in childhood or adolescence, involves the immune system mistakenly attacking and destroying insulin-producing cells. Consequently, individuals with Type 1 diabetes often require a carefully managed balance of insulin injections and a well-considered diet. In contrast, Type 2 diabetes, often linked to lifestyle factors, obesity, and genetic predisposition, may initially be managed through lifestyle modifications, including dietary adjustments.

Navigating the intricacies of diabetes involves a nuanced understanding of how various foods affect blood sugar levels. Carbohydrates, for instance, have a direct impact on blood glucose, requiring careful consideration in meal planning. Fibre-rich foods, such as whole grains and vegetables, can contribute to stable blood sugar levels, while sugary and processed foods may lead to undesirable spikes.

Managing blood sugar levels through diet is of paramount importance in diabetes care. An overview of this critical aspect emphasizes the need for individuals to adopt a proactive and informed approach to their dietary choices. Balancing macronutrients, monitoring portion sizes, and making informed decisions about the glycaemic index of foods are key strategies in achieving optimal blood sugar control.

In essence, comprehending the basics of diabetes and its intersection with dietary choices provides a foundation for individuals to proactively manage their condition. This understanding sets the stage for the exploration of more advanced concepts and strategies in the ongoing journey towards effective diabetes management.

Key Components of a Diabetic Diet

In crafting an effective diabetic diet, understanding the nuanced roles of key macronutrients-carbohydrates, proteins, fats, and fiber-is paramount. This section delves into the significance of each component and their collective impact on blood sugar levels for individuals managing diabetes.

1. Carbohydrates:
Quality Matters: Emphasise complex carbohydrates with a low glycemic index, such as whole grains, legumes, and vegetables. These choices release glucose gradually, preventing sudden spikes in blood sugar.
Portion Awareness: Be mindful of carbohydrate portions, considering their direct influence on blood glucose levels. Consistent carbohydrate intake throughout the day aids in better blood sugar management.

2. Proteins:
Lean and Satisfying: Prioritise lean protein sources like fish, poultry, tofu, and legumes. Protein contributes to satiety, supporting weight management, and has minimal impact on blood sugar levels.

3. Fats:

Healthy Choices: Opt for unsaturated fats found in avocados, nuts, seeds, and olive oil. These fats offer cardiovascular benefits without compromising blood lipid levels, crucial for individuals with diabetes.

Moderation is Key: Practice moderation in fat consumption, balancing intake for overall health without excessive caloric load.

4. Fiber:

Digestive Health: Include a variety of fiber-rich foods, such as fruits, vegetables, and whole grains. Fiber aids digestion, promotes a feeling of fullness, and helps control blood sugar levels.

Balancing Nutrients: The combination of fiber with other macronutrients in meals can contribute to a more gradual release of glucose into the bloodstream.

Glycemic Index and Meal Planning:

Understanding Impact: The glycemic index (GI) measures how quickly a carbohydrate-containing food raises blood glucose levels. Foods with a lower GI are generally preferable, as they lead to a slower, more controlled increase in blood sugar.

Strategic Meal Choices: Incorporate lower-GI foods in meal planning to help manage blood sugar levels. Combining different macronutrients strategically can further modulate the overall glycemic impact of a meal.

Portion Control and Mindful Eating:

Optimal Portions: Practise portion control to avoid overconsumption of calories and carbohydrates. Smaller, balanced portions contribute to better blood sugar regulation.

Mindful Choices: Engage in mindful eating by paying attention to hunger and fullness cues. This approach fosters a positive relationship with food, encourages healthier choices, and supports overall well-being.

Understanding the intricate interplay of carbohydrates, proteins, fats, and fiber, along with incorporating the glycemic index into meal planning, forms the foundation of a well-rounded diabetic diet. Combined with portion control and mindful eating practices, this holistic approach empowers individuals to make informed choices that positively impact their blood sugar levels and overall health.

Building a Balanced Plate

Creating a balanced plate is an art that combines nutritional wisdom with diabetes-specific considerations. This section provides practical guidelines and tips for constructing meals that are both well-balanced and tailored to the needs of individuals managing diabetes.

Guidelines for Creating Well-Balanced Meals:

Vegetables as the Foundation:

Fill half your plate with a vibrant array of non-starchy vegetables. These nutrient-rich options are low in calories, high in fibre, and provide essential vitamins and minerals.

Moderate Portions of Lean Proteins:

Include a moderate portion of lean protein, such as fish, poultry, tofu, or legumes. Protein supports satiety, muscle health, and assists in blood sugar control without causing significant spikes.

Whole Grains for Sustained Energy:

Allocate a quarter of your plate to whole grains like brown rice, quinoa, or whole-grain pasta. These complex carbohydrates release glucose gradually, providing a steady source of energy.

Healthy Fats in Moderation:

Incorporate sources of healthy fats, such as avocados, nuts, and olive oil, in moderation. These fats contribute to overall well-being without compromising blood lipid levels.

Mindful Use of Carbohydrates:

Choose carbohydrates with a low glycemic index to help manage blood sugar levels. Be mindful of portion sizes and spread carbohydrate intake evenly throughout the day.

Tips for Incorporating Variety in Diabetes-Friendly Meals:

Experiment with Different Vegetables:
Explore a variety of non-starchy vegetables to add colour, flavour, and diverse nutrients to your meals. Rotate through options like leafy greens, bell peppers, broccoli, and cauliflower.

Diversify Protein Sources:
Mix up protein sources to keep meals interesting. Incorporate fish, lean meats, plant-based proteins, and dairy products to ensure a well-rounded intake of essential amino acids.

Explore Whole Grain Alternatives:
Experiment with different whole grains to add texture and variety. Try options like quinoa, bulgur, barley, or whole-grain couscous as alternatives to traditional refined grains.

Include a Rainbow of Fruits:
Incorporate a variety of fruits to provide natural sweetness and a spectrum of vitamins and antioxidants. Berries, citrus fruits, and apples are excellent choices with a lower impact on blood sugar.

Spice Up Flavours with Herbs and Spices:
Enhance the taste of your meals with herbs and spices instead of excessive salt or sugar. Experiment with basil, oregano, cumin, or cinnamon to add depth without compromising health.

Plan Ahead for Balanced Snacks:
Prepare balanced snacks that combine protein and fibre to keep blood sugar levels steady between meals. Nuts with a piece of fruit or Greek yogurt with berries are nutritious options.

Stay Hydrated with Water:
Make water your primary beverage to stay hydrated without adding extra calories or sugars. Herbal teas or infused water can provide additional flavour without compromising health.

By following these guidelines and incorporating a variety of foods, individuals can create balanced plates that cater to their nutritional needs while managing diabetes effectively. This approach not only supports blood sugar control but also ensures a diverse and enjoyable culinary experience.

Managing Special Diabetic Considerations

Effectively managing diabetes involves considering various factors beyond blood sugar levels. This section explores the impact of other health conditions on the diabetic diet, provides guidance on alcohol consumption, and offers strategies for dining out and social situations while adhering to dietary needs.

1. Impact of Health Conditions:

- Heart Health Considerations: Individuals with diabetes often face an increased risk of cardiovascular issues. Adopting heart-healthy dietary practices, such as incorporating unsaturated fats, limiting saturated fats and cholesterol, and prioritising whole foods, can support overall cardiovascular well-being.
- Kidney Health Awareness: Kidney health is another critical aspect for those managing diabetes. Monitoring and moderating protein intake, staying adequately hydrated, and managing blood pressure contribute to kidney health alongside diabetes care.

2. Guidance for Alcohol Consumption:

- Moderation is Key: Moderate alcohol consumption can be a part of a diabetic diet, but it requires careful consideration. Limiting alcohol intake to moderate levels, defined as up to one drink per day for women and up to two drinks per day for men, is generally considered safe.
- Effect on Blood Sugar: Alcohol can influence blood sugar levels, and consuming it on an empty stomach may lead to hypoglycemia. It is advisable to monitor blood sugar levels regularly and consume alcohol with food to mitigate its impact.

3. Strategies for Dining Out and Social Situations:

- Menu Exploration: When dining out, explore menu options in advance and choose restaurants that offer a variety of nutritious choices. Opt for grilled, baked, or steamed dishes, and inquire about ingredient substitutions or modifications.
- Portion Awareness: Restaurants often serve larger portions than necessary. Consider sharing a dish, ordering an appetizer as a main course, or requesting a half portion to maintain portion control.
- Carry Healthy Snacks: When attending social events, bring along diabetes-friendly snacks to ensure there are nutritious options available. This

helps manage hunger and prevents overindulgence in less healthy choices.
- Effective Communication: Informing friends and family about dietary needs can make social situations more accommodating. It's helpful to communicate dietary restrictions in advance to facilitate supportive environments.
- Mindful Eating at Gatherings: Practise mindful eating by savouring each bite, being aware of portion sizes, and paying attention to hunger and fullness cues. This approach supports a positive relationship with food in social settings.
- Stay Active: Incorporate physical activity into social gatherings, such as taking a post-meal walk. This not only aids in blood sugar management but also promotes overall well-being.

By addressing these special considerations, individuals can enhance their ability to manage diabetes effectively, taking into account the impact of other health conditions, navigating alcohol consumption responsibly, and adopting strategies to maintain a balanced diabetic diet in various social situations.

Monitoring and Adjusting

Regular blood sugar monitoring is a cornerstone of effective diabetes management, providing valuable insights into individual responses to dietary choices. This section underscores the importance of monitoring, offers tips for making informed adjustments to the diet, and emphasizes the collaborative role of healthcare professionals in tailoring dietary plans to personal needs.

1. Importance of Regular Blood Sugar Monitoring:

- ◆ Dynamic Nature of Diabetes: Diabetes is a dynamic condition influenced by various factors, including diet, physical activity, stress, and medication. Regular blood sugar monitoring offers a real-time understanding of how these factors impact blood glucose levels.
- ◆ Informed Decision-Making: Monitoring blood sugar levels allows individuals to make informed decisions about their dietary choices. It provides a basis for identifying patterns, recognizing the effects of specific foods, and making timely adjustments to maintain optimal blood sugar control.
- ◆ Prevention of Complications: Regular monitoring plays a crucial role in preventing long-term complications associated with uncontrolled blood sugar levels. Timely intervention and adjustments contribute to overall well-being and reduce the risk of complications.

2. Tips for Making Adjustments Based on Individual Responses:

- ◆ Keep a Food Diary: Maintaining a food diary helps track dietary choices and their impact on blood sugar levels. This documentation aids in identifying trends and making targeted adjustments to the diet.
- ◆ Observe Patterns: Pay attention to how different foods, portion sizes, and meal timings affect blood sugar levels. Identifying patterns enables individuals to make specific and personalised adjustments to their dietary plan.
- ◆ Experiment with Timing: Experimenting with meal timing can be beneficial. For some individuals, eating smaller, more frequent meals may help stabilise blood sugar levels, while others may find success with larger meals spread further apart.
- ◆ Consult Healthcare Professionals: Seek guidance from healthcare professionals, including dietitians and diabetes educators, when making significant adjustments. Their expertise ensures that modifications align with overall health goals and do not compromise nutritional needs.

3. Working with Healthcare Professionals to Tailor the Diet:

- ◆ Collaborative Approach: Diabetes management is a collaborative effort between individuals and healthcare professionals. Work closely with dietitians and healthcare providers to tailor the diet to personal needs, considering factors like medica-

tion, physical activity, and individual preferences.
- ◆ Regular Check-Ins: Schedule regular check-ins with healthcare professionals to review blood sugar trends, discuss dietary challenges, and make necessary adjustments. These check-ins provide ongoing support and fine-tune the dietary plan as needed.
- ◆ Holistic Assessment: Healthcare professionals take a holistic approach to diabetes care, considering not only blood sugar levels but also other health parameters. This comprehensive evaluation ensures that the dietary plan aligns with overall health objectives.

By placing a strong emphasis on regular blood sugar monitoring, making informed adjustments based on individual responses, and collaborating with healthcare professionals, individuals with diabetes can proactively manage their condition. This approach fosters a personalised and effective dietary plan that promotes optimal blood sugar control and contributes to long-term well-being.

Lifestyle Factors and the Diabetic Diet

Recognising the intricate interplay between lifestyle factors and the diabetic diet is essential for comprehensive diabetes management. This section explores the roles of physical activity, stress management, and adequate sleep in fostering a healthy diabetic lifestyle.

1. The Role of Physical Activity in Blood Sugar Management:
- ✓ Enhanced Insulin Sensitivity: Engaging in regular physical activity enhances insulin sensitivity, allowing cells to effectively use glucose for energy. This can lead to improved blood sugar control and a reduced need for insulin or oral medications.
- ✓ Aerobic and Resistance Exercises: Incorporating a combination of aerobic exercises (such as brisk walking or cycling) and resistance training (weightlifting or bodyweight exercises) provides comprehensive benefits. These activities contribute to overall fitness, weight management, and better blood sugar regulation.
- ✓ Consistent Routine: Establishing a consistent exercise routine is crucial. Regular physical activity helps maintain stable blood sugar levels and promotes cardiovascular health, reducing the risk of complications associated with diabetes.

2. Managing Stress and Its Impact on Dietary Choices:
- ✓ Stress and Blood Sugar Levels: Chronic stress can elevate blood sugar levels as the body releases stress hormones like cortisol. Adopting stress management techniques, such as mindfulness, deep breathing, or yoga, can positively influence blood sugar control.
- ✓ Mindful Eating Practices: Stress can lead to emotional eating and unhealthy food choices. Practising mindful eating, being aware of hunger and fullness cues, and choosing nutritious foods can help individuals manage stress without compromising their dietary goals.
- ✓ Incorporating Relaxation Techniques: Integrating relaxation techniques into daily life, such as meditation or regular breaks for leisure activities, aids in stress reduction. This, in turn, supports overall well-being and contributes to a healthier lifestyle.

3. Adequate Sleep and Its Connection to a Healthy Diabetic Lifestyle:
- ✓ Quality Sleep and Blood Sugar Control: Poor sleep patterns and insufficient sleep duration can disrupt hormonal balance, leading to insulin resistance and increased hunger. Prioritising quality sleep supports blood sugar management and overall metabolic health.
- ✓ Establishing a Sleep Routine: Creating a consistent sleep routine, including a regular bedtime and a calming pre-sleep ritual, helps regulate the body's internal clock. Adequate sleep contributes to better energy levels and cognitive function, facilitating healthier lifestyle choices.
- ✓ Addressing Sleep Disorders: Individuals with diabetes should address any sleep disorders promptly, such as sleep apnoea, which can impact blood sugar control. Seeking medical advice and adopting strategies to improve sleep quality is vital for a holistic diabetic lifestyle.

By recognising the influence of physical activity, stress management, and adequate sleep on blood sugar control, individuals with diabetes can adopt a holistic approach to their lifestyle. Integrating these factors with a well-balanced diet enhances overall well-being, empowers individuals in their diabetes management, and reduces the risk of complications associated with the condition.

Practical Tips

Embarking on a diabetic diet involves not only understanding nutritional principles but also implementing practical strategies in everyday activities. This section provides practical tips for grocery shopping, meal preparation, and cooking to support individuals in managing their diabetes effectively.

1. Grocery Shopping:

- ⋄ Plan Ahead: Create a shopping list based on your meal plan to avoid impulsive purchases. Planning ahead ensures that you have the necessary ingredients for balanced and diabetes-friendly meals.
- ⋄ Focus on Fresh Produce: Prioritise fresh fruits and vegetables, aiming for a variety of colours and types. These nutrient-rich foods form the foundation of a healthy diabetic diet.
- ⋄ Read Food Labels: Be vigilant about reading food labels to identify hidden sugars, excessive salt, and unhealthy fats. Look for whole, unprocessed options and choose products with lower glycemic index values.
- ⋄ Shop the Perimeter: The perimeter of the grocery store typically houses fresh produce, lean proteins, and dairy. Concentrate on these areas to incorporate wholesome, unprocessed items into your diet.

2. Meal Preparation:

- ⋄ Batch Cooking: Prepare larger quantities of meals and freeze individual portions for future use. This simplifies meal planning, ensures variety, and minimises the temptation to opt for less healthy convenience options.
- ⋄ Include a Balance of Nutrients: Each meal should consist of a balance of carbohydrates, proteins, and healthy fats. Preparing meals that encompass a variety of nutrients supports overall health and aids in blood sugar control.
- ⋄ Experiment with Herbs and Spices: Enhance the flavour of your dishes with herbs and spices instead of relying on excessive salt or sugar. Experimenting with different seasonings adds variety without compromising health.
- ⋄ Smart Cooking Techniques: Choose cooking methods such as baking, grilling, or steaming over frying. These techniques retain the nutritional value of foods while minimizing added fats.

3. Cooking for a Diabetic Diet:

- ⋄ Control Portion Sizes: Use smaller plates to help control portion sizes. Measuring and portioning out ingredients during meal preparation ensures that you are mindful of calorie and carbohydrate intake.
- ⋄ Choose Healthy Cooking Oils: Opt for heart-healthy oils like olive oil or avocado oil when cooking. These fats contribute to a balanced diet without negatively impacting blood lipid levels.
- ⋄ Monitor Cooking Temperatures: Pay attention to cooking temperatures, especially when grilling or roasting. Avoid excessive charring or browning, which can introduce potentially harmful compounds.
- ⋄ Incorporate Whole Grains: Substitute refined grains with whole grains like brown rice, quinoa, or whole-grain pasta. These choices offer more fibre and nutrients, contributing to better blood sugar management.

Adopting these practical tips into your daily routine can help simplify the process of adhering to a diabetic diet. By making informed choices during grocery shopping, embracing efficient meal preparation strategies, and incorporating healthy cooking practices, individuals can navigate their dietary requirements with ease, promoting overall well-being and effective diabetes management.

Chapter 2: Breakfast

Protein Spinach Waffles

PREP TIME: 2 MINUTES, COOK TIME: 5 MINUTES, MAKES: 2 WAFFLES

- 1½ tbsps. extra-virgin olive oil, divided
- 2 large eggs, beaten
- 30 g baby spinach
- 60 g ground almonds
- 30 g tapioca flour
- ½ tsp. baking soda
- ¼ tsp. pink salt
- ¼ tsp. oregano (optional)
- ¼ tsp. garlic powder (optional)

1. In a nonstick frying pan, heat ½ tbsp. of olive oil over medium heat.
2. Add the spinach and cook for about 3 minutes until spinach wilts. Keep aside.
3. In a bowl, combine the eggs, the remaining tbsp. of olive oil, tapioca flour, ground almonds, baking soda, salt, oregano and garlic powder (if using). Mix to blend well.
4. Gently stir in the spinach.
5. Make the waffles according to your waffle maker instructions. Enjoy!

Nutrition Info per Serving:
Calories: 427, Protein: 14 g, Fat: 36 g, Carbohydrates: 14 g, Fibre: 3 g, Sugar: 1 g, Sodium: 424 mg

French Asparagus and Courgette Omelette

PREP TIME: 16 MINUTES, COOK TIME: 4 HOURS, SERVES: 6

- 12 eggs, beaten
- 140 g chopped fresh asparagus
- 1 small courgette, peeled and diced
- 1 yellow pepper, stemmed, seeded, and chopped
- 60 g grated low-fat Parmesan cheese
- 80 ml semi-skimmed milk
- 2 shallots, peeled and minced
- ½ tsp. dried tarragon leaves
- ½ tsp. dried thyme leaves
- ¼ tsp. salt

1. Grease the inside of a 6.5-litre crockpot lightly with plain vegetable oil.
2. Mix the eggs, milk, thyme, tarragon, and salt in a large bowl, and mix well with an eggbeater or wire whisk until well combined.
3. Place the asparagus, courgette, yellow pepper, and shallots. Put into the crockpot.
4. Cover the crockpot and cook on low for 3 to 4 hours, or until the eggs are set.
5. Scatter with the Parmesan cheese, cover and cook for another 5 to 10 minutes or until the cheese starts to melt. Enjoy!

Nutrition Info per Serving:
Calories: 236, Protein: 18 g, Fat: 13 g, Carbohydrates: 9 g, Fibre: 2 g, Sugar: 4 g, Sodium: 394 mg

Homemade Cinnamon Rolls

🕒 PREP TIME: 16 MINUTES, COOK TIME: 25 MINUTES, MAKES: 10 ROLLS

For the Dough:
- 3 tbsps. coconut oil, plus more for greasing the pan
- 300-350 g wholemeal pastry flour, divided
- 250 ml unsweetened almond milk
- 1 packet instant yeast or rapid-rise yeast
- 1 tbsp. erythritol
- ¼ tsp. sea salt

For the Filling:
- 3 tbsps. melted coconut oil
- 50 g erythritol
- 2 tbsps. pure maple syrup
- 1½ tbsps. ground cinnamon

For the Frosting:
- 2½ tbsps. pure maple syrup
- 375 ml low-fat Greek yoghurt
- 1 tsp. vanilla extract
- ½ tsp. maple extract

Make the Dough:

1. In a large saucepan, heat the almond milk, erythritol, and coconut oil until warm and melted, but not boiling. Take the mixture from the heat, and allow it to cool for 5 minutes. Transfer the milk mixture to a large mixing bowl, and scatter the yeast across the surface. Let it sit for about 10 minutes to allow the yeast to activate.
2. Add the salt and 50 g flour to the bowl, and stir it in. Continue to add the remaining flour, 50 g at a time, stirring as you go. The dough will be sticky. Once the dough is too thick to stir, take it to a lightly floured surface, and knead it for a minute or so, until it forms a loose ball (be careful not to overmix). Continue to add flour a little at a time, as needed, until the dough no longer sticks to your hands. You may not need all the flour. Knead the dough for about 5 minutes, or until all the flour is entirely incorporated and the dough is smooth and springy.
3. Take the dough back to the bowl, cover it with clingfilm or a clean dish towel, and place it in a warm place to rise for 1 hour, or until it is doubled in size.

Make the Filling:

4. In a small bowl, combine the erythritol and cinnamon. Combine the coconut oil and the maple syrup in a separate small bowl. Keep the bowls aside.
5. Grease an 20-cm square pan lightly with coconut oil.
6. On a lightly floured surface, gently roll out the dough into a thin, even 0.5-cm rectangle. Brush with the coconut oil and maple syrup mixture. Then, generously scatter with the erythritol and cinnamon mixture.
7. Starting at one end, tightly roll up the dough and situate it seam side down. Cut the dough into ten 2-3-cm sections with a serrated knife. Layer the rolls in the prepared pan.
8. Allow the rolls to rise while you preheat the oven to 180°C.
9. Once the oven is hot, bake the rolls until very slightly golden brown, for about 18 to 20 minutes. Pay close attention so they do not overcook and get too dry. Let the rolls cool in the pan for 10 minutes. While the rolls are cooling, prepare the frosting. Stir together the yoghurt, vanilla, maple syrup, and maple extract. Spread the frosting on top of the rolls. Enjoy!

Nutrition Info per Serving:

Calories: 305, Protein: 8 g, Fat: 12 g, Carbohydrates: 42 g, Fibre: 5 g, Sugar: 5 g, Sodium: 75 mg

Apples and Walnuts Porridge

PREP TIME: 4 MINUTES, COOK TIME: 35 MINUTES, SERVES: 4

- Coconut oil spray (optional)
- 2 apples, peeled, cored, and halved
- 160 g coarse oatmeal
- 500 ml water
- 4 tbsps. chopped walnuts
- 1 tsp. cinnamon

1. Preheat the oven to 190ºC.
2. Place the apples cut-side up on a small baking sheet, then lightly spray with coconut oil (if using), and scatter with cinnamon.
3. Bake for about 15 minutes, or until tender.
4. Meanwhile, bring the water to a boil in a small saucepan.
5. Place the coarse oatmeal, reduce the heat to low, cover, and cook for 20 minutes.
6. Remove from the heat and keep aside.
7. In each of 4 serving bowls, add a quarter of the porridge, ½ apple, and a tbsp. of walnuts on top.

Nutrition Info per Serving:
Calories: 317, Protein: 7 g, Fat: 12 g, Carbohydrates: 51 g, Fibre: 8 g, Sugar: 16 g, Sodium: 6 mg

Spicy Shakshuka

PREP TIME: 8 MINUTES, COOK TIME: 10 MINUTES, SERVES: 2

- 3 tbsps. extra-virgin olive oil
- 4 large eggs
- 3 colourful peppers (green, yellow, red), cubed
- 120 g crushed tomatoes
- ½ brown onion, finely chopped
- 30 g crumbled feta
- Avocado (optional)
- Fresh parsley (optional)
- ¼ tsp. pink salt
- ¼ tsp. basil (optional)
- ¼ tsp. oregano (optional)
- Freshly ground black pepper (optional)

1. In a large frying pan, heat the olive oil over medium heat.
2. Add the onion and peppers, cover, and cook for 2 minutes.
3. Place the crushed tomatoes, salt, oregano, basil, and black pepper (if using). Cover and cook for about 5 minutes, until most of the liquid evaporates.
4. Use a slotted spoon to move the veggies around, making 4 circles in between the veggies where you can drop in the eggs. Gently crack an egg into each circle and cover the pan with a lid. Cook for 2 minutes for a runny yolk, or longer if you prefer them more well done.
5. Once the eggs are done, place some crumbled feta on top. Turn off the heat, cover, and allow the dish to rest for 1 or 2 minutes, until the feta melts.
6. Put some avocado and fresh parsley on top (if using), and serve warm.

Nutrition Info per Serving:
Calories: 455, Protein: 17 g, Fat: 38 g, Carbohydrates: 18 g, Fibre: 6 g, Sugar: 10 g, Sodium: 637 mg

Cheese Spinach Omelette

⏱ PREP TIME: 3 MINUTES, COOK TIME: 6 MINUTES, SERVES: 1

- 1 tbsp. extra-virgin olive oil
- 2 large eggs, beaten
- 30 g baby spinach, roughly chopped
- 1 spring onion (green and white parts), finely chopped
- 1 tbsp. low-fat goat's cheese
- ¼ tsp. pink salt
- Freshly ground black pepper (optional)
- ¼ tsp. oregano (optional)

1. In a nonstick frying pan, heat the olive oil over medium heat.
2. Add the spring onions and cook for 1 minute, until wilted.
3. Place the spinach and cook for 1 minute more.
4. Put the beaten eggs, salt, pepper, and oregano (if using). Stir to combine well and cook on low heat until the bottom of the omelette seems firm.
5. Add the goat's cheese and carefully fold the omelette in half with a wide spatula.
6. Cook for about 1 minute, then flip over and cook for an additional minute.
7. Serve hot.

Nutrition Info per Serving:
Calories: 369, Protein: 21 g, Fat: 30 g, Carbohydrates: 4 g, Fibre: 1 g, Sugar: 1 g, Sodium: 648 mg

....

Baked Eggs with Zoodles

⏱ PREP TIME: 4 MINUTES, COOK TIME: 7 MINUTES, SERVES: 2

- 2 tbsps. extra-virgin olive oil
- 2 large eggs
- 1 courgette, spiralised and patted dry
- ½ small red onion, finely sliced
- 1 tsp. chives, finely chopped
- ¼ tsp. pink salt
- Freshly ground black pepper (optional)
- ¼ tsp. oregano (optional)

1. In a medium frying pan, heat the olive oil over medium heat.
2. Add the onion and sauté until soft and translucent.
3. Place the courgette, oregano (if using), and salt. Cook for about 2 minutes.
4. Using a slotted spoon, move the courgette to make 2 circles where you can drop in the eggs. Put the eggs and cover. Cook for another 2 minutes for a runny yolk, or longer if you prefer them more well done.
5. Sprinkle with the fresh chives and black pepper, if desired.
6. Serve hot.

Nutrition Info per Serving:
Calories: 232, Protein: 7 g, Fat: 20 g, Carbohydrates: 5 g, Fibre: 1.5 g, Sugar: 2.5 g, Sodium: 318 mg

Egg and Mushroom Wild Rice Casserole

PREP TIME: 15 MINUTES, COOK TIME: 7 HOURS, SERVES: 6 TO 8

- 11 eggs
- 540 g plain cooked wild rice
- 200 g sliced mushrooms
- 180 g shredded low-fat Emmental cheese
- 1 red pepper, stemmed, seeded, and chopped
- 1 onion, minced
- 2 garlic cloves, minced
- 1 tsp. dried thyme leaves
- ¼ tsp. salt

1. Layer the wild rice, mushrooms, red pepper, onion, and garlic in a 6.5-litre crockpot.
2. Beat the eggs with the thyme and salt in a large bowl. Pour into the crockpot. Place the cheese on top.
3. Cover the crockpot and cook on low for 5 to 7 hours, or until a food thermometer registers 75°C and the casserole is set. Serve warm.

Nutrition Info per Serving:
Calories: 330, Protein: 19 g, Fat: 18 g, Carbohydrates: 24 g, Fibre: 3 g, Sugar: 2 g, Sodium: 380 mg

Coconut Quinoa Breakfast Porridge

PREP TIME: 8 MINUTES, COOK TIME: 15 MINUTES, SERVES: 2

- ¼ tsp. extra-virgin coconut oil
- 1 tsp. cinnamon, ground
- 90 g quinoa, rinsed
- 125 ml almond milk
- 125 ml light coconut milk
- 2 drops liquid stevia
- 1 tbsp. unsweetened desiccated coconut
- 150 g blueberries

1. In a medium pan, heat the oil and cinnamon over medium-high heat for about 1 minute.
2. Add the quinoa and toss to coat.
3. Pour the almond milk and coconut milk. Bring to a boil.
4. Lower the heat so the mixture simmers. Cover the pan.
5. Continue to simmer until the quinoa has absorbed all the milk, about 10 minutes.
6. Stir in the stevia.
7. Top with coconut and blueberries and serve

Nutrition Info per Serving:
Calories: 352, Protein: 8 g, Fat: 15 g, Carbohydrates: 47 g, Fibre: 7 g, Sugar: 8 g, Sodium: 105 mg

Savoury Turkey Patties

PREP TIME: 6 MINUTES, COOK TIME: 10 MINUTES, SERVES: 4

- 500 g extra-lean minced turkey breast
- 1 small apple, peeled, cored, and diced small
- 2 large spring onions, chopped finely
- 1 fresh jalapeño pepper, seeded and chopped finely
- 1 tbsp. fresh ginger, grated
- 1 tbsp. fresh coriander, chopped
- Pinch of sea salt
- Pinch of black pepper, freshly ground
- 1 tbsp. olive oil

1. Combine all the ingredients in a medium bowl except the oil until very well mixed.
2. Form the turkey mixture into 8 patties, 7-cm in diameter per patty.
3. In a large frying pan over medium heat, heat the oil and cook the patties until golden and cooked through, about 4 minutes per side.
4. Serve with greens or a hard-boiled egg.

Nutrition Info per Serving:
Calories: 234, Protein: 34 g, Fat: 10 g, Carbohydrates: 4 g, Fibre: 1 g, Sugar: 2 g, Sodium: 176 mg

Chapter 3: Grain and Rice

Wild Rice with Parsley

PREP TIME: 5 MINUTES, COOK TIME: 6 HOURS, SERVES: 8

- 540 g wild rice, rinsed and drained
- 1.5 L vegetable broth
- 1 onion, chopped
- 10 g chopped fresh flat-leaf parsley
- 1 bay leaf
- ½ tsp. dried thyme leaves
- ½ tsp. dried basil leaves
- ½ tsp. salt

1. Mix the wild rice, vegetable broth, onion, salt, thyme, basil, and bay leaf in a 6.5 litre crockpot. Cover the crockpot and cook on low for 4 to 6 hours, or until the wild rice is tender but still firm. You can cook this longer until the wild rice pops that will take about 7 to 8 hours.
2. Remove the bay leaf and discard.
3. Toss in the parsley and serve warm.

Nutrition Info per Serving:
Calories: 247, Protein: 7 g, Fat: 1 g, Carbohydrates: 52 g, Fibre: 5 g, Sugar: 2 g, Sodium: 811 mg

....

Mint and Pea Risotto

PREP TIME: 5 MINUTES, COOK TIME: 20 MINUTES, SERVES: 2

- 2 tbsps. coconut oil
- 1 onion, peeled and diced
- ½ tsp. garlic powder
- 90 g barley
- 250 ml vegetable broth, divided
- Salt and pepper, to taste
- 60 g fresh peas
- ¼ tsp. lime zest
- 5 g chopped fresh mint leaves

1. Press the Sauté button on the Instant Pot and heat the oil.
2. Add the onion and stir-fry for 5 minutes.
3. Add garlic powder and barley and cook for 1 minute more.
4. Pour in 125 ml vegetable broth and stir for 3 minutes until it is absorbed by barley.
5. Add the remaining 125 ml broth, salt, and pepper.
6. Secure the lid. Select the Manual mode and set the cooking time for 10 minutes at High Pressure.
7. Once cooking is complete, do a natural pressure release for 10 minutes, then release any remaining pressure. Carefully open the lid.
8. Stir in peas, lime zest, and mint and let sit for 3 minutes until heated through. Serve immediately.

Nutrition Info per Serving:
Calories: 399, Protein: 7 g, Fat: 15 g, Carbohydrates: 58 g, Fibre: 10 g, Sugar: 4 g, Sodium: 596 mg

Couscous with Balsamic Dressing

⏲ PREP TIME: 10 MINUTES, COOK TIME: 5 MINUTES, SERVES: 6

For the Dressing:
- 60 ml extra-virgin olive oil
- 2 tbsps. balsamic vinegar
- 2 drops liquid stevia
- Sea salt and freshly ground black pepper, to taste

For the Couscous:
- 200 g wholewheat couscous
- Pinch sea salt
- 1 tsp. almond butter
- 500 ml boiling water
- 1 spring onion, white and green parts, chopped
- 60 g chopped pecans
- 2 tbsps. chopped fresh parsley

To Make the Dressing
1. Whisk together the oil, vinegar, and stevia.
2. Season with salt and pepper and set it aside.
- To Make the Couscous
3. Put the couscous, salt, and almond butter in a large heat-proof bowl and pour the boiling water on top. Stir and cover the bowl. Let it sit for 5 minutes. Uncover and fluff the couscous with a fork.
4. Stir in the dressing, spring onion, pecans, and parsley.
5. Serve warm.

Nutrition Info per Serving:
Calories: 293, Protein: 6 g, Fat: 16 g, Carbohydrates: 32 g, Fibre: 4 g, Sugar: 1 g, Sodium: 86 mg

Mushroom Spelt Bowl

⏲ PREP TIME: 10 MINUTES, COOK TIME: 18 TO 19 MINUTES, SERVES: 2

- 1 tbsp. olive oil
- 1 onion, chopped
- 70 g sliced mushrooms
- 1 sweet pepper, chopped
- 1 garlic clove, minced
- 125 ml white wine
- 375 ml vegetable broth
- 150 g wholegrain spelt
- Sea salt and ground black pepper, to taste
- 30 g grated low-fat Emmental cheese
- 1 tbsp. chopped fresh parsley

1. Set the Instant Pot on the Sauté mode and heat the oil. Add the onion to the pot and sauté for 3 to 4 minutes, or until softened. Add the mushrooms and pepper and sauté for 3 minutes. Stir in the garlic and continue to sauté for 1 minute.
2. Pour in the white wine to deglaze the pan. Stir in the vegetable broth, spelt, salt and black pepper.
3. Lock the lid, select the Manual mode and set the cooking time for 11 minutes on High Pressure. When the timer goes off, do a natural pressure release for 10 minutes, then release any remaining pressure. Open the lid.
4. Transfer the dish to bowls and serve topped with the cheese and fresh parsley.

Nutrition Info per Serving:
Calories: 472, Protein: 15 g, Fat: 11 g, Carbohydrates: 78 g, Fibre: 14 g, Sugar: 9 g, Sodium: 598 mg

Chapter 3: Grain and Rice / 15

Nut Buckwheat Pilaf

PREP TIME: 10 MINUTES, COOK TIME: 11 MINUTES, SERVES: 4

- 1 tbsp. olive oil
- 4 garlic cloves, minced
- 1 red pepper, diced
- 550 ml chicken broth
- 160 g roasted buckwheat
- 100 g yellow split peas
- ¾ tsp. dried thyme
- Salt and black pepper, to taste
- 175 g chopped dried figs
- 60 g toasted walnuts
- 15 g chopped coriander

1. Press the Sauté button on the Instant Pot and heat the oil. Add the garlic and red pepper to the pot and sauté for 5 minutes. Stir in the chicken broth, buckwheat, yellow split peas, thyme, salt and pepper.
2. Close and secure the lid. Select the Manual mode and set the cooking time for 6 minutes on High Pressure. Once the timer goes off, use a natural pressure release for 10 minutes, then release any remaining pressure. Carefully open the lid.
3. Stir in the figs, walnuts and coriander. Spoon the pilaf into bowls and enjoy.

Nutrition Info per Serving:
Calories: 384, Protein: 12 g, Fat: 11 g, Carbohydrates: 62 g, Fibre: 12 g, Sugar: 14 g, Sodium: 512 mg

Apple and Pecan Quinoa Salad

PREP TIME: 7 MINUTES, COOK TIME: 8 MINUTES, SERVES: 4 TO 6

- 180 g quinoa, rinsed
- 250 ml water
- ¼ tsp. salt, plus more as needed
- 2 apples, unpeeled and cut into large dices
- 2 tbsps. freshly squeezed lemon juice
- 1 tbsp. white rice vinegar
- 2 celery sticks, halved lengthwise and chopped
- ½ bunch spring onions, green and light green parts, sliced
- 150-180 g dried cranberries, white raisins, and regular raisins
- 2 tbsps. avocado oil
- ½ to 1 tsp. chilli powder, plus more as needed
- Pinch freshly ground black pepper
- 60-120 g chopped pecans
- 15 g chopped fresh coriander

1. Combine the quinoa, water, and salt in the Instant Pot.
2. Secure the lid. Select the Manual mode and set the cooking time for 8 minutes at High Pressure.
3. Once cooking is complete, do a natural pressure release for 10 minutes, then release any remaining pressure. Carefully open the lid.
4. Transfer the quinoa to a large salad bowl. Refrigerate for 5 minutes to cool.
5. Mix the apples, lemon juice, and vinegar in a small resealable container. Cover and shake lightly to coat the apples, then refrigerate.
6. Remove the cooled quinoa and stir in the celery, spring onions, cranberry-raisin mix, oil, and chilli powder. Taste and season with more salt and pepper, as needed. Add the apples and lemon-vinegar juice into the salad and stir well.
7. Serve topped with the pecans and coriander.

Nutrition Info per Serving:
Calories: 402, Protein: 7 g, Fat: 18 g, Carbohydrates: 57 g, Fibre: 7 g, Sugar: 26 g, Sodium: 108 mg

Spelt and Cherry Salad

PREP TIME: 5 MINUTES, COOK TIME: 40 MINUTES, SERVES: 4 TO 6

- 750 ml water
- 200 g wholegrain spelt, rinsed
- 1 tbsp. extra-virgin olive oil
- 1 tbsp. apple cider vinegar
- 300 g cherries, cut into halves
- 25 g chopped spring onions
- 1 tsp. lemon juice
- Salt, to taste
- 10 mint leaves, chopped

1. Combine the water and spelt in the Instant Pot.
2. Lock the lid. Select the Manual mode and set the cooking time for 40 minutes at High Pressure.
3. When the timer beeps, perform a quick pressure release. Carefully remove the lid.
4. Drain the spelt and transfer to a bowl. Stir in the olive oil, vinegar, cherries, spring onions, lemon juice, salt, and mint. Serve immediately.

Nutrition Info per Serving:
Calories: 349, Protein: 7 g, Fat: 8 g, Carbohydrates: 65 g, Fibre: 11 g, Sugar: 5 g, Sodium: 615 mg

---

Pearl Barley with Peppers

PREP TIME: 5 MINUTES, COOK TIME: 25 MINUTES, SERVES: 2

- 1 tbsp. sesame oil
- ½ brown onion, chopped
- 1 garlic clove, minced
- 1 red pepper, deseeded and chopped
- 1 jalapeño pepper, deseeded and chopped
- 375 ml vegetable broth
- 135 g pearl barley, rinsed
- 2 tbsps. chopped chives

1. Set the Instant Pot to the Sauté mode and heat the oil. Add the onion to the pot and sauté for 3 minutes, or until just tender and fragrant. Add the garlic, red pepper and jalapeño pepper to the pot and sauté for 2 minutes, or until fragrant. Stir in the vegetable broth and pearl barley.
2. Lock the lid. Select the Multigrain mode and set the cooking time for 20 minutes on High Pressure. When the timer goes off, perform a quick pressure release. Carefully open the lid.
3. Fluff the pearl barley mixture with a fork. Serve garnished with the chopped chives.

Nutrition Info per Serving:
Calories: 349, Protein: 7 g, Fat: 8 g, Carbohydrates: 65 g, Fibre: 11 g, Sugar: 5 g, Sodium: 615 mg

---

Quinoa with Spinach

PREP TIME: 5 MINUTES, COOK TIME: 2 MINUTES, SERVES: 4

- 270 g quinoa, rinsed
- 375 ml water
- 120 g spinach
- 1 red pepper, chopped
- 3 celery sticks, chopped
- ¼ tsp. salt

1. Combine all ingredients in the Instant Pot.
2. Secure the lid. Select the Manual mode and set the cooking time for 2 minutes at High Pressure.
3. Once cooking is complete, do a natural pressure release for 10 minutes, then release any remaining pressure. Carefully open the lid.
4. Fluff the quinoa and serve.

Nutrition Info per Serving:
Calories: 248, Protein: 9 g, Fat: 3 g, Carbohydrates: 47 g, Fibre: 6 g, Sugar: 2 g, Sodium: 161 mg

---

Blueberry Wild Rice

PREP TIME: 15 MINUTES, COOK TIME: 45 MINUTES, SERVES: 4

- 1 tbsp. extra-virgin olive oil
- ½ sweet onion, chopped
- 625 ml sodium-free chicken broth
- 180 g wild rice, rinsed and drained
- Pinch sea salt
- 65 g toasted pumpkin seeds
- 75 g blueberries
- 1 tsp. chopped fresh basil

1. Place a medium saucepan over medium-high heat and add the oil.
2. Sauté the onion until softened and translucent, about 3 minutes.
3. Stir in the broth and bring to a boil.
4. Stir in the rice and salt and reduce the heat to low. Cover and simmer until the rice is tender, about 40 minutes.
5. Drain off any excess broth, if necessary. Stir in the pumpkin seeds, blueberries, and basil.
6. Serve warm.

Nutrition Info per Serving:
Calories: 287, Protein: 9 g, Fat: 9 g, Carbohydrates: 44 g, Fibre: 4 g, Sugar: 5 g, Sodium: 66 mg

Chapter 4: Noodles and Pasta

Turkey Spaghetti

⏱ PREP TIME: 10 MINUTES, COOK TIME: 16 MINUTES, SERVES: 4 TO 6

- 1 tsp. olive oil
- 500 g minced turkey
- 1 clove garlic, minced
- ¼ onion, diced
- 225 g wholemeal spaghetti, halved
- 1 jar (800-g) tomato-basil sauce
- ¾ tsp. coarse salt
- 500 ml water
- shredded low-fat Parmesan cheese (optional)

1. Set your Instant Pot to Sauté. Add and heat the oil.
2. Add the minced turkey and sauté for 3 minutes.
3. Fold in the garlic and onion. Sauté for another 4 minutes.
4. Mix in the spaghetti, sauce and salt. Add the water to the pot and stir to combine.
5. Secure the lid. Press the Manual button on the Instant Pot and cook for 9 minutes on High Pressure.
6. Once the cooking is complete, do a quick pressure release. Carefully remove the lid.
7. Serve topped with the shredded cheese.

Nutrition Info per Serving:
Calories: 454, Protein: 32 g, Fat: 10 g, Carbohydrates: 56 g, Fibre: 10 g, Sugar: 12 g, Sodium: 722 mg

Chicken Fettuccine Alfredo

⏱ PREP TIME: 5 MINUTES, COOK TIME: 3 MINUTES, SERVES: 2

- 225 g wholemeal fettuccine, halved
- 500 ml water
- 2 tsps. chicken seasoning
- 150 g cooked and diced chicken
- 1 jar (450-g) Alfredo sauce
- Salt and ground black pepper, to taste

1. Add the pasta, water, and chicken seasoning to the Instant Pot and stir to combine.
2. Secure the lid. Press the Manual button on the Instant Pot and set the cooking time for 3 minutes at High Pressure.
3. When the timer goes off, perform a quick pressure release. Carefully remove the lid.
4. Drain the pasta and transfer to a serving bowl.
5. Add the cooked chicken and drizzle the sauce over the top. Sprinkle with salt and pepper.
6. Stir until well mixed and serve.

Nutrition Info per Serving:
Calories: 629, Protein: 38 g, Fat: 23 g, Carbohydrates: 68 g, Fibre: 10 g, Sugar: 6 g, Sodium: 778 mg

Minced Beef Pasta

🕐 PREP TIME: 5 MINUTES, COOK TIME: 11 TO 13 MINUTES, SERVES: 4

- 1 tsp. olive oil
- 500 g minced beef
- 250 g dried wholemeal pasta
- 700 g pasta sauce
- 375 ml water
- Salt and ground black pepper, to taste
- Italian seasoning, to taste

1. Press the Sauté button on the Instant Pot. Add the oil and let heat for 1 minute.
2. Fold in the minced beef and cook for 3 to 5 minutes until browned, stirring frequently.
3. Mix in the pasta, sauce and water and stir to combine.
4. Secure the lid. Press the Manual button on the Instant Pot and set the cooking time for 7 minutes on High Pressure.
5. Once cooking is complete, do a quick pressure release. Carefully remove the lid.
6. Stir in salt, pepper, and Italian seasoning and stir well.
7. Transfer to a serving dish and serve immediately.

Nutrition Info per Serving:
Calories: 625, Protein: 31 g, Fat: 16 g, Carbohydrates: 88 g, Fibre: 14 g, Sugar: 11 g, Sodium: 753 mg

Caper and Olive Pasta

🕐 PREP TIME: 10 MINUTES, COOK TIME: 5 MINUTES, SERVES: 4

- 3 cloves garlic, minced
- 400 g wholemeal short pasta such as penne or fusilli
- 1 L homemade or store-bought pasta sauce
- 750 ml water, plus more as needed
- 1 tbsp. capers
- 80 g Kalamata olives, sliced
- ¼ tsp. crushed red pepper flakes
- Salt and pepper, to taste

1. Press the Sauté button on your Instant Pot and add the garlic.
2. Add a splash of water and cook for about 30 seconds until fragrant.
3. Mix in the pasta, pasta sauce, water, capers, olives, and crushed red pepper flakes and stir to combine.
4. Lock the lid. Press the Manual button on the Instant Pot and set the cooking time for 5 minutes on High Pressure.
5. Once the timer goes off, use a quick pressure release. Carefully remove the lid.
6. Fold in the pasta and sprinkle with salt and pepper. Stir well.
7. Serve immediately.

Nutrition Info per Serving:
Calories: 479, Protein: 14 g, Fat: 4 g, Carbohydrates: 96 g, Fibre: 12 g, Sugar: 14 g, Sodium: 700 mg

Spinach and Mushroom Pasta

⏱ PREP TIME: 5 MINUTES, COOK TIME: 10 MINUTES, SERVES: 4

- 1 tbsp. oil
- 230 g mushrooms, minced
- ½ tsp. coarse salt
- ½ tsp. black ground pepper
- 230 g uncooked wholemeal spaghetti pasta
- 420 ml water
- 150 g spinach
- 125 ml homemade pesto
- 25 g grated low-fat Parmesan cheese

1. Press the Sauté button on the Instant Pot and heat the oil. Add the mushrooms, salt and pepper to the pot and sauté for 5 minutes. Add the pasta and water.
2. Set the lid in place. Select the Manual mode and set the cooking time for 5 minutes on High Pressure. When the timer goes off, do a quick pressure release. Carefully open the lid.
3. Stir in the spinach, pesto, and cheese. Serve immediately.

Nutrition Info per Serving:
Calories: 348, Protein: 13 g, Fat: 15 g, Carbohydrates: 42 g, Fibre: 6 g, Sugar: 2 g, Sodium: 452 mg

Cherry Tomato Farfalle with Pesto

⏱ PREP TIME: 5 MINUTES, COOK TIME: 8 TO 9 MINUTES, SERVES: 2 TO 4

- 150 g wholemeal farfalle
- 1 L water
- 180 ml vegan pesto sauce
- 150 g cherry tomatoes, quartered

1. Place the farfalle and water in your Instant Pot.
2. Secure the lid. Press the Manual button and cook for 7 minutes at High Pressure.
3. Once cooking is complete, do a quick pressure release. Carefully remove the lid.
4. Drain the pasta and transfer it back to the pot.
5. Stir in the sauce.
6. Press the Sauté button on your Instant Pot and cook for 1 to 2 minutes.
7. Fold in the tomatoes and stir to combine.
8. Transfer to a serving dish and serve immediately.

Nutrition Info per Serving:
Calories: 386, Protein: 10 g, Fat: 22 g, Carbohydrates: 38 g, Fibre: 5 g, Sugar: 3 g, Sodium: 340 mg

Creamy Tomato Pasta with Spinach

PREP TIME: 5 MINUTES, COOK TIME: 9 MINUTES, SERVES: 4

- 1 (800-g) can crushed tomatoes
- 300 g wholemeal penne, rotini, or fusilli
- 1 tbsp. dried basil
- ½ tsp. garlic powder
- ½ tsp. salt, plus more as needed
- 375 ml water
- 250 ml unsweetened coconut milk
- 60 g chopped fresh spinach (optional)
- Freshly ground black pepper, to taste

1. Combine the tomatoes, pasta, basil, garlic powder, salt, and water in the Instant Pot.
2. Secure the lid. Select the Manual mode and set the cooking time for 4 minutes at High Pressure.
3. Once cooking is complete, do a natural pressure release for 5 minutes, then release any remaining pressure. Carefully open the lid.
4. Stir in the milk and spinach (if desired). Taste and season with more salt and pepper, as needed.
5. Set your Instant Pot to Sauté and let cook for 4 to 5 minutes, or until the sauce is thickened and the greens are wilt. Serve warm.

Nutrition Info per Serving:
Calories: 434, Protein: 11 g, Fat: 9 g, Carbohydrates: 79 g, Fibre: 10 g, Sugar: 9 g, Sodium: 461 mg

. . . .

Basil Tomato Pasta

PREP TIME: 10 MINUTES, COOK TIME: 10 MINUTES, SERVES: 4

- 1 tsp. olive oil, plus more for drizzling
- 1 large Spanish onion, diced
- 300 g wholemeal penne, rotini, or fusilli
- 500 ml water
- 30 g sun-dried tomatoes, chopped
- ½ tsp. salt, plus more as needed
- 150 g cherry tomatoes, halved or quartered
- 2 tbsps. finely chopped fresh basil
- ½ tsp. garlic powder (optional)
- Freshly ground black pepper, to taste

1. Set your Instant Pot to Sauté and heat 1 tsp. of olive oil.
2. Add the onion and sauté for 4 to 5 minutes, stirring occasionally, until the onion is tender.
3. Add the pasta, water, tomatoes, and a pinch of salt. Stir well.
4. Secure the lid. Select the Manual mode and set the cooking time for 4 minutes at High Pressure.
5. Once cooking is complete, do a natural pressure release for 5 minutes, then release any remaining pressure. Carefully open the lid.
6. Set your Instant Pot to Sauté again and stir in the cherry tomatoes, basil, garlic powder (if desired), and another drizzle of olive oil.
7. Taste and season with more salt and pepper, as needed. Serve warm.

Nutrition Info per Serving:
Calories: 335, Protein: 10 g, Fat: 3 g, Carbohydrates: 68 g, Fibre: 10 g, Sugar: 7 g, Sodium: 357 mg

Penne Pasta with Tomato-Vodka Sauce

PREP TIME: 5 MINUTES, COOK TIME: 4 MINUTES, SERVES: 2

- 50 g uncooked wholemeal penne pasta
- 120 g crushed tomatoes
- 250 ml water
- 30 ml coconut oil
- 1 tbsp. vodka
- 1 tsp. garlic powder
- ½ tsp. salt
- ¼ tsp. paprika
- 125 ml coconut cream
- 2 g minced coriander

1. Add all the ingredients, except for the coconut cream and coriander, to the Instant Pot and stir to combine.
2. Set the lid in place. Select the Manual mode and set the cooking time for 4 minutes on High Pressure. When the timer goes off, do a quick pressure release. Carefully open the lid.
3. Stir in the coconut cream and fresh coriander and serve hot.

Nutrition Info per Serving:
Calories: 481, Protein: 6 g, Fat: 35 g, Carbohydrates: 38 g, Fibre: 7 g, Sugar: 6 g, Sodium: 626 mg

....

Sesame Noodle and Courgette Bowl

PREP TIME: 4 MINUTES, COOK TIME: 15 MINUTES, SERVES: 2

- 3 tbsps. sesame oil, divided
- 1 L water
- 1 courgette, cut into small slices
- 125 g brown rice noodles
- 2 Thai chillies
- 6 garlic cloves, minced
- Juice of ½ lime
- ½ tsp. minced fresh ginger
- ¼ tsp. toasted sesame seeds
- Sea salt
- Freshly ground black pepper

1. In a large pot over high heat, bring the water to a boil. Place the brown rice noodles and stir, leaving the heat on high and the pot uncovered, cooking for about 10 minutes. Drain the water from the pot.
2. When the noodles are cooking, heat 2 tbsps. of sesame oil over medium heat in a large frying pan. Put the courgette, garlic, and Thai chillies, and cook for about 5 minutes, until the courgette begins to soften.
3. Once the noodles have finished cooking, place them to the large frying pan and mix to combine with the sesame oil mixture.
4. Stir in the lime juice, ginger, and remaining 1 tbsp. of sesame oil. Sprinkle with salt and pepper.
5. Divide the noodles equally between 2 bowls and garnish with the toasted sesame seeds. Enjoy!

Nutrition Info per Serving:
Calories: 575, Protein: 9 g, Fat: 30 g, Carbohydrates: 72 g, Fibre: 4 g, Sugar: 4 g, Sodium: 384 mg

Chapter 5: Bean and Legumes

Herbed Black Beans

⏱ PREP TIME: 11 MINUTES, COOK TIME: 9 HOURS, SERVES: 8

- 600 g dried black beans, rinsed and drained
- 1.5 L low-sodium vegetable broth
- 2 onions, chopped
- 8 garlic cloves, minced
- 1 tsp. dried basil leaves
- ½ tsp. dried thyme leaves
- ½ tsp. dried oregano leaves
- ½ tsp. salt

1. Mix all the ingredients in a 6.5-litre crockpot. Cover the crockpot and cook on low for 7 to 9 hours, or until the beans have absorbed the liquid and are tender.
2. Remove the bay leaf and discard.

Nutrition Info per Serving:
Calories: 275, Protein: 15 g, Fat: 1 g, Carbohydrates: 52 g, Fibre: 13 g, Sugar: 2 g, Sodium: 303 mg

....

Chickpeas Curry

⏱ PREP TIME: 15 MINUTES, COOK TIME: 35 MINUTES, SERVES: 4

- 200 g dried chickpeas
- 1 tbsp. baking soda
- 1 L water, divided
- 1 tsp. olive oil
- 1 clove garlic, minced
- 30 g diced onion
- ½ tsp. hot curry powder
- ¼ tsp. ground cinnamon
- 1 bay leaf
- ½ tsp. sea salt

1. Add the chickpeas, baking soda, and 500 ml water to a large bowl and soak for 1 hour. Rinse the chickpeas and drain.
2. In the Instant Pot, heat the oil on Sauté mode. Add the garlic and onion and sauté for 3 minutes.
3. Add the curry, cinnamon, and bay leaf and stir well. Stir in the chickpeas and 500 ml water.
4. Cover the lid. Select Manual mode and set cooking time for 32 minutes on High Pressure.
5. When timer beeps, use a natural pressure release for 15 minutes, then release any remaining pressure.
6. Remove the lid and stir in the sea salt. Remove the bay leaf before serving.

Nutrition Info per Serving:
Calories: 193, Protein: 9 g, Fat: 4 g, Carbohydrates: 33 g, Fibre: 7 g, Sugar: 6 g, Sodium: 595 mg

Rosemary White Beans with Onion

⏱ PREP TIME: 8 MINUTES, COOK TIME: 8 HOURS, SERVES: 16

- 500 g cannellini beans
- 500 ml low sodium vegetable broth
- 1 L water
- 1 onion, finely chopped
- 3 cloves garlic, minced
- 1 large sprig fresh rosemary
- ½ tsp. salt
- ⅛ tsp. white pepper

1. Sort over the beans, remove and discard any extraneous material. Rinse the beans well over cold water and drain.
2. In a 6.5-litre crockpot, combine the beans, onion, garlic, rosemary, salt, water, and vegetable broth.
3. Cover the crockpot and cook on low for 6 to 8 hours or until the beans are soft.
4. Remove and discard the rosemary stem. Stir in the mixture gently and serve warm.

Nutrition Info per Serving:
Calories: 127, Protein: 7 g, Fat: 1 g, Carbohydrates: 24 g, Fibre: 6 g, Sugar: 1 g, Sodium: 117 mg

Green Lentil and Carrot Stew

⏱ PREP TIME: 5 MINUTES, COOK TIME: 30 MINUTES, SERVES: 4

- 2 tbsps. extra-virgin olive oil
- 400 g green lentils, rinsed
- 1 carrot, chopped
- 2 celery sticks, chopped
- 1 brown onion, chopped
- 1.5 L water
- 1 tsp. pink salt
- 1 tbsp. cumin (optional)
- Freshly ground black pepper (optional)

1. In a frying pan, heat the oil over medium heat. Place the carrots, celery, and onion. Cook until the onion is translucent.
2. Place the lentils, salt, cumin (if using), and water. Stir, cover, reduce the heat to low, and sauté for about 25 to 30 minutes.
3. Season with more salt and black pepper, if desired. Serve right away.

Nutrition Info per Serving:
Calories: 379, Protein: 24 g, Fat: 8 g, Carbohydrates: 54 g, Fibre: 24 g, Sugar: 4 g, Sodium: 568 mg

Mexican Black Bean and Chicken Soup

⏲ PREP TIME: 10 MINUTES, COOK TIME: 25 MINUTES, SERVES: 7

- 2 tbsps. olive oil
- ½ onion, diced
- 500 g boneless and skinless chicken breast, cut into 1-cm cubes
- ½ tsp. Adobo seasoning, divided
- ¼ tsp. black pepper
- 1 (400-g) can no-salt-added black beans, rinsed and drained
- 1 400-g) can fire-roasted tomatoes
- 70 g frozen corn
- ½ tsp. cumin
- 1 tbsp. chilli powder
- 1.2 L low-sodium chicken broth

❶ Grease a stockpot with olive oil and heat over medium-high heat until shimmering.
❷ Add the onion and sauté for 3 minutes or until translucent.
❸ Add the chicken breast and sprinkle with Adobo seasoning and pepper. Put the lid on and cook for 6 minutes or until lightly browned. Shake the pot halfway through the cooking time.
❹ Add the remaining ingredients. Reduce the heat to low and simmer for 15 minutes or until the black beans are soft.
❺ Serve immediately.

Nutrition Info per Serving:
Calories: 231, Protein: 21 g, Fat: 7 g, Carbohydrates: 21 g, Fibre: 6 g, Sugar: 4 g, Sodium: 284 mg

---

Lentils with Spinach

⏲ PREP TIME: 15 MINUTES, COOK TIME: 15 MINUTES, SERVES: 2

- 1 tbsp. olive oil
- ½ tsp. cumin seeds
- ¼ tsp. mustard seeds
- 3 cloves garlic, finely chopped
- 1 green chilli, finely chopped
- 1 large tomato, chopped
- 45 g spinach, finely chopped
- ¼ tsp. turmeric powder
- ½ tsp. salt
- 50 g yellow split peas, rinsed
- 50 g red lentils, rinsed
- 375 ml water
- ¼ tsp. garam masala
- 2 tsps. lemon juice
- coriander, for garnish

❶ Press the Sauté button on the Instant Pot. Add the oil and then the cumin seeds and mustard seeds.
❷ Let the seeds sizzle for a few seconds and then add the garlic and green chilli. Sauté for 1 minute or until fragrant.
❸ Add the tomato and cook for 1 minute. Add the chopped spinach, turmeric powder and salt, and cook for 2 minutes.
❹ Add the rinsed peas and lentils and stir. Pour in the water and put the lid on.
❺ Press the Manual button and set the cooking time for 10 minutes on High Pressure.
❻ When timer beeps, let the pressure release naturally for 5 minutes, then release any remaining pressure.
❼ Open the pot and add the garam masala, lemon juice and coriander. Serve immediately.

Nutrition Info per Serving:
Calories: 321, Protein: 17 g, Fat: 8 g, Carbohydrates: 49 g, Fibre: 18 g, Sugar: 4 g, Sodium: 595 mg

Black Bean and Tomato Soup with Lime Yoghurt

PREP TIME: 8 HOURS 10 MINUTES, COOK TIME: 1 HOUR 33 MINUTES, SERVES: 8

- 2 tbsps. avocado oil
- 1 medium onion, chopped
- 1 (300-g) can diced tomatoes and green chillies
- 500 g dried black beans, soaked in water for at least 8 hours, rinsed
- 1 tsp. ground cumin
- 3 garlic cloves, minced
- 1.5 L chicken bone broth, vegetable broth, or water
- coarse salt, to taste
- 1 tbsp. freshly squeezed lime juice
- 60 ml unsweetened Greek yoghurt

1. Heat the avocado oil in a nonstick frying pan over medium heat until shimmering.
2. Add the onion and sauté for 3 minutes or until translucent.
3. Transfer the onion to a pot, then add the tomatoes and green chillies and their juices, black beans, cumin, garlic, broth, and salt. Stir to combine well.
4. Bring to a boil over medium-high heat, then reduce the heat to low. Simmer for 1 hour and 30 minutes or until the beans are soft.
5. Meanwhile, combine the lime juice with Greek yoghurt in a small bowl. Stir to mix well.
6. Pour the soup in a large serving bowl, then drizzle with lime yoghurt before serving.

Nutrition Info per Serving:
Calories: 315, Protein: 18 g, Fat: 7 g, Carbohydrates: 49 g, Fibre: 14 g, Sugar: 4 g, Sodium: 539 mg

Easy Three-Bean Medley

PREP TIME: 16 MINUTES, COOK TIME: 8 HOURS, SERVES: 10

- 250 g dried black beans, rinsed and drained
- 250 g dried kidney beans, rinsed and drained
- 250 g dried black-eyed beans, rinsed and drained
- 2 carrots, peeled and chopped
- 1.5 L low-sodium vegetable broth
- 375 ml water
- 1 onion, chopped
- 1 leek, chopped
- 2 garlic cloves, minced
- ½ tsp. dried thyme leaves

1. Mix all of the ingredients in a 6.5-litre crockpot. Cover with lid and cook on low for 6 to 8 hours, or until the beans are soft and the liquid is absorbed. Serve warm.

Nutrition Info per Serving:
Calories: 196, Protein: 11 g, Fat: 1 g, Carbohydrates: 38 g, Fibre: 11 g, Sugar: 3 g, Sodium: 200 mg

Black-Eyed Beans with Collard

PREP TIME: 5 MINUTES, COOK TIME: 3 TO 4 MINUTES, SERVES: 4 TO 6

- 1 brown onion, diced
- 1 tbsp. olive oil
- 200 g dried black-eyed beans
- 25 g chopped sun-dried tomatoes
- 60 ml tomato purée
- 1 tsp. smoked paprika
- 50 ml water
- 4 large collard green leaves
- Salt and freshly ground black pepper, to taste

1. In the Instant Pot, select Sauté mode. Add the onion and olive oil and cook for 3 to 4 minutes, stirring occasionally, until the onion is softened.
2. Add the black-eyed beans, tomatoes, tomato purée, paprika, water, and stir to combine.
3. Close the lid, then select Manual mode and set cooking time for 30 minutes on High Pressure.
4. Once the cook time is complete, let the pressure release naturally for about 15 minutes, then release any remaining pressure.
5. Trim off the thick parts of the collard green stems, then slice the leaves lengthwise in half or quarters. Roll them up together, then finely slice into ribbons.
6. Sprinkle the sliced collard greens with salt and massage it into them with hands to soften.
7. Open the lid. Add the collard greens and ½ tsp. of salt to the pot, stirring to combine and letting the greens wilt in the heat.
8. Serve immediately.

Nutrition Info per Serving:
Calories: 208, Protein: 9 g, Fat: 5 g, Carbohydrates: 33 g, Fibre: 7 g, Sugar: 4 g, Sodium: 417 mg

Adzuki Bean and Celery Soup

PREP TIME: 6 MINUTES, COOK TIME: 35 MINUTES, SERVES: 4 TO 6

- 30 ml extra-virgin olive oil
- 2 (400-g) cans adzuki beans, drained and rinsed
- 1 large carrot, finely diced
- 1 long celery stick, finely diced
- 1 leek, chopped
- 1 small brown onion, finely chopped
- 1.5 L water
- 1½ tsps. pink salt
- 2 bay leaves (optional)

1. In a medium saucepan, heat the olive oil over medium heat. Place the leeks, onions, carrots, and celery. Cook for 5 minutes.
2. Put the salt and bay leaves (if using), then pour in the beans and water.
3. Cover and cook over medium-low heat for 30 minutes, until some of the water evaporates and the vegetables are cooked through. If you like thinner stew, shorten the cook time a little.
4. Remove and discard the bay leaves. Serve immediately.

Nutrition Info per Serving:
Calories: 221, Protein: 10 g, Fat: 7 g, Carbohydrates: 31 g, Fibre: 11 g, Sugar: 3 g, Sodium: 781 mg

Chapter 6: Fish and Seafood

Cod with Asparagus

PREP TIME: 15 MINUTES, COOK TIME: 11 MINUTES, SERVES: 2

- 2 (170 g) boneless cod fillets
- 2 tbsps. fresh parsley, roughly chopped
- 2 tbsps. fresh dill, roughly chopped
- 1 bunch asparagus
- 1 tsp. dried basil
- 1½ tbsps. fresh lemon juice
- 1 tbsp. olive oil
- Salt and black pepper, to taste

1. Preheat the Air fryer to 205ºC and grease an Air fryer basket.
2. Mix lemon juice, oil, parsley, dill, basil, salt, and black pepper in a small bowl.
3. Combine the cod and ¾ of the oil mixture in another bowl.
4. Coat asparagus with remaining oil mixture and transfer to the Air fryer basket.
5. Roast for about 3 minutes and arrange cod fillets on top of asparagus.
6. Roast for about 8 minutes and dish out in serving plates.

Nutrition Info per Serving:
Calories: 302, Protein: 36 g, Fat: 13 g, Carbohydrates: 10 g, Fibre: 4 g, Sugar: 3 g, Sodium: 211 mg

Spicy Prawns

PREP TIME: 15 MINUTES, COOK TIME: 5 MINUTES, SERVES: 3

- 500 g prawns, peeled and deveined
- 2 tbsps. olive oil
- 1 tsp. old bay seasoning
- ½ tsp. red chilli flakes
- ½ tsp. smoked paprika
- ½ tsp. cayenne pepper
- Salt, as required

1. Preheat the Air fryer to 200ºC and grease an Air fryer basket.
2. Mix the prawns with olive oil and other seasonings in a large bowl.
3. Arrange the prawns into the Air fryer basket in a single layer and roast for about 5 minutes.
4. Dish out the prawns onto serving plates and serve hot.

Nutrition Info per Serving:
Calories: 228, Protein: 34 g, Fat: 9 g, Carbohydrates: 1 g, Fibre: 0 g, Sugar: 0 g, Sodium: 256 mg

Chinese Style Cod

⏱ PREP TIME: 20 MINUTES, COOK TIME: 15 MINUTES, SERVES: 2

- 2 (200 g) cod fillets
- 250 ml water
- 2 spring onions (green part), sliced
- 10 g fresh coriander, chopped
- Salt and black pepper, to taste
- ¼ tsp. sesame oil
- 1 tsp. erythritol
- 5 tbsps. light soy sauce
- 1 tsp. dark soy sauce
- 3 tbsps. olive oil
- 5 ginger slices

1. Preheat the Air fryer to 180ºC and grease an Air fryer basket.
2. Season each cod fillet with salt and black pepper and drizzle with sesame oil.
3. Arrange the cod fillets into the Air fryer basket and air fry for about 12 minutes.
4. Bring water to boil and add erythritol and both soy sauces.
5. Cook until erythritol is dissolved, continuously stirring and keep aside.
6. Dish out the cod fillets onto serving plates and top each fillet with coriander and spring onions.
7. Heat olive oil over medium heat in a small frying pan and add ginger slices.
8. Sauté for about 3 minutes and discard the ginger slices.
9. Drizzle the hot oil over cod fillets and top with the sauce mixture to serve.

Nutrition Info per Serving:
Calories: 382, Protein: 35 g, Fat: 25 g, Carbohydrates: 5 g, Fibre: 1 g, Sugar: 0 g, Sodium: 1031 mg

Thai Fish Curry

⏱ PREP TIME: 6 MINUTES, COOK TIME: 6 MINUTES, SERVES: 6

- 700 g salmon fillets
- 500 ml fresh coconut milk
- 10 g chopped coriander
- 80 ml olive oil
- 2 tbsps. curry powder
- Salt and pepper, to taste

1. In the Instant Pot, add all the ingredients. Give a good stir.
2. Lock the lid. Select the Manual mode and set the cooking time for 6 minutes at Low Pressure.
3. Once cooking is complete, do a quick pressure release. Carefully open the lid. Set warm.

Nutrition Info per Serving:
Calories: 436, Protein: 32 g, Fat: 33 g, Carbohydrates: 3 g, Fibre: 1 g, Sugar: 0 g, Sodium: 88 mg

Chapter 6: Fish and Seafood

Simple Salmon

PREP TIME: 5 MINUTES, COOK TIME: 10 MINUTES, SERVES: 2

- 2 (170 g) salmon fillets
- Salt and black pepper, as required
- 1 tbsp. olive oil

1. Preheat the Air fryer to 200ºC and grease an Air fryer basket.
2. Season each salmon fillet with salt and black pepper and drizzle with olive oil.
3. Arrange salmon fillets into the Air fryer basket and roast for about 10 minutes.
4. Remove from the Air fryer and dish out the salmon fillets onto the serving plates.

Nutrition Info per Serving:
Calories: 328, Protein: 34 g, Fat: 20 g, Carbohydrates: 0 g, Fibre: 0 g, Sugar: 0 g, Sodium: 66 mg

Cod Cakes

PREP TIME: 20 MINUTES, COOK TIME: 14 MINUTES, SERVES: 6

- 500 g cod fillet
- 1 egg
- 30 g coconut, grated and divided
- 1 spring onion, finely chopped
- 2 tbsps. fresh parsley, chopped
- 1 tsp. fresh lime zest, finely grated
- 1 tsp. red chilli paste
- Salt, as required
- 1 tbsp. fresh lime juice

1. Preheat the Air fryer to 190ºC and grease an Air fryer basket.
2. Put the cod fillet, lime zest, egg, chilli paste, salt and lime juice in a food processor and pulse until smooth.
3. Transfer the cod mixture into a bowl and add spring onion, parsley and 2 tbsps. of coconut.
4. Mix until well combined and make 12 equal-sized round cakes from the mixture.
5. Place the remaining coconut in a shallow bowl and coat the cod cakes with coconut.
6. Arrange cod cakes into the Air fryer basket in 2 batches and bake for about 7 minutes.
7. Dish out in 2 serving plates and serve warm.

Nutrition Info per Serving:
Calories: 149, Protein: 20 g, Fat: 6 g, Carbohydrates: 3 g, Fibre: 1 g, Sugar: 0 g, Sodium: 186 mg

Breaded Flounder

PREP TIME: 15 MINUTES, COOK TIME: 12 MINUTES, SERVES: 3

- 1 egg
- 120 g panko breadcrumbs
- 3 (170 g) flounder fillets
- 1 lemon, sliced
- 60 ml vegetable oil

1. Preheat the Air fryer to 180ºC and grease an Air fryer basket.
2. Whisk the egg in a shallow bowl and mix breadcrumbs and oil in another bowl.
3. Dip flounder fillets into the whisked egg and coat with the breadcrumb mixture.
4. Arrange flounder fillets into the Air fryer basket and air fry for about 12 minutes.
5. Dish out the flounder fillets onto serving plates and garnish with the lemon slices to serve.

Nutrition Info per Serving:
Calories: 391, Protein: 28 g, Fat: 18 g, Carbohydrates: 28 g, Fibre: 1 g, Sugar: 2 g, Sodium: 383 mg

Sesame Seeds Coated Haddock

PREP TIME: 15 MINUTES, COOK TIME: 14 MINUTES, SERVES: 4

- 4 tbsps. coconut flour
- 2 eggs
- 75 g sesame seeds, toasted
- 60 g panko breadcrumbs
- 4 (170 g) frozen haddock fillets
- ⅛ tsp. dried rosemary, crushed
- Salt and ground black pepper, as required
- 3 tbsps. olive oil

1. Preheat the Air fryer to 200ºC and grease an Air fryer basket.
2. Place the flour in a shallow bowl and whisk the eggs in a second bowl.
3. Mix sesame seeds, breadcrumbs, rosemary, salt, black pepper and olive oil in a third bowl until a crumbly mixture is formed.
4. Coat each fillet with flour, dip into whisked eggs and finally, dredge into the breadcrumb mixture.
5. Arrange haddock fillets into the Air fryer basket in a single layer and roast for about 14 minutes, flipping once in between.
6. Dish out the haddock fillets onto serving plates and serve hot.

Nutrition Info per Serving:
Calories: 413, Protein: 25 g, Fat: 29 g, Carbohydrates: 16 g, Fibre: 3 g, Sugar: 1 g, Sodium: 395 mg

Thyme-Sesame Crusted Halibut

PREP TIME: 6 MINUTES, COOK TIME: 8 MINUTES, SERVES: 4

- 250 ml water
- 1 tsp. dried thyme leaves
- 1 tbsp. toasted sesame seeds
- 230 g halibut, sliced
- Salt and pepper, to taste
- 1 tbsp. freshly squeezed lemon juice

1. Set a trivet in the Instant Pot and pour the water into the pot.
2. Season the halibut with lemon juice, salt, and pepper. Sprinkle with dried thyme leaves and sesame seeds.
3. Place the fish on the trivet.
4. Lock the lid. Select the Steam mode and cook for 8 minutes at Low Pressure.
5. Once cooking is complete, do a quick pressure release. Carefully open the lid.
6. Serve warm.

Nutrition Info per Serving:
Calories: 80, Protein: 16 g, Fat: 2 g, Carbohydrates: 0 g, Fibre: 0 g, Sugar: 0 g, Sodium: 52 mg

Tuna Salad with Lettuce

PREP TIME: 12 MINUTES, COOK TIME: 10 MINUTES, SERVES: 4

- 2 tbsps. olive oil
- 230 g tuna, sliced
- 1 tbsp. fresh lemon juice
- 2 eggs
- 1 head lettuce
- Salt and pepper, to taste
- 250 ml water

1. In a large bowl, season the tuna with lemon juice, salt and pepper. Transfer the tuna to a baking dish.
2. Add the eggs, water, and steamer rack to the Instant Pot. Place the baking dish on the steamer rack.
3. Lock the lid. Select the Steam mode and set the cooking time for 10 minutes at Low Pressure.
4. Once cooking is complete, do a quick pressure release. Carefully open the lid.
5. Allow the eggs and tuna to cool. Peel the eggs and slice into wedges. Set aside.
6. Assemble the salad by shredding the lettuce in a salad bowl. Toss in the cooled tuna and eggs.
7. Sprinkle with olive oil, then serve.

Nutrition Info per Serving:
Calories: 184, Protein: 20 g, Fat: 10 g, Carbohydrates: 4 g, Fibre: 2 g, Sugar: 2 g, Sodium: 189 mg

Chapter 7: Vegetables

Perfect Roasted Brussels Sprouts

⏲ PREP TIME: 5 MINUTES, COOK TIME: 20 MINUTES, SERVES: 4

- 700 g Brussels sprouts, trimmed and halved
- 2 tbsps. olive oil
- ¼ tsp. salt
- ½ tsp. freshly ground black pepper

1. Preheat the oven to 205°C.
2. Combine the Brussels sprouts and olive oil in a large mixing bowl and toss until they are evenly coated.
3. Turn the Brussels sprouts out onto a large baking sheet and flip them over so they are cut-side down with the flat part touching the baking sheet. Sprinkle with salt and pepper.
4. Bake for 20 to 30 minutes or until the Brussels sprouts are lightly charred and crisp on the outside and toasted on the bottom. The outer leaves will be extra dark, too.
5. Serve immediately.

Nutrition Info per Serving:
Calories: 125, Protein: 5 g, Fat: 7 g, Carbohydrates: 14 g, Fibre: 6 g, Sugar: 3 g, Sodium: 170 mg

Sautéed Cabbage

⏲ PREP TIME: 5 MINUTES, COOK TIME: 20 MINUTES, SERVES: 4 TO 6

- 2 tbsps. olive oil
- 1 medium green cabbage (about 600 g), cored and chopped well
- 1 red onion, chopped well
- 15 g freshly chopped parsley
- 1½ tsps. lemon juice
- 1 tbsp. balsamic vinegar
- Salt and black pepper

1. Put cabbage in a large bowl and add cold water to cover. about 3 minutes, drained off.
2. Heat 1 tbsp. oil in a large nonstick frying pan over medium-high heat (180°C to 205°C) until until it begins to glisten and shimmer. Add onion and ¼ tsp. salt and cook until tender and lightly browned, 5 to 7 minutes, remove to a large bowl.
3. Heat remaining 1 tbsp. oil in frying pan over medium-high heat until it begins to shimmer. Add cabbage and spread with ½ tsp. salt and ¼ tsp. pepper to season. Cover and cook, without stirring, until cabbage is wilted and lightly browned on bottom, about 3 minutes. Uncovered, Stirring periodically and cook, until cabbage is crisp-tender and lightly browned, about 4 minutes, stirring once halfway through the cooking time.
4. Remove from heat, whisk in parsley, onion, vinegar and lemon juice. Sprinkle with salt and pepper to season and serve warm.

Nutrition Info per Serving:
Calories: 135, Protein: 2 g, Fat: 7 g, Carbohydrates: 18 g, Fibre: 6 g, Sugar: 9 g, Sodium: 321 mg

Low-Carb Cauliflower Mash

PREP TIME: 10 MINUTES, COOK TIME: 10 MINUTES, SERVES: 4

- 1 tbsp. olive oil
- 1 head cauliflower (about 1.4 kg), trimmed and cut into florets
- 4 garlic cloves
- 4 L water (enough to cover cauliflower)
- 2 tsps. dried parsley
- ¼ tsp. salt
- ⅛ tsp. freshly ground black pepper

1. Bring a large pot of water to a boil. Add the cauliflower and garlic. Cook for about 10 minutes or until the cauliflower is fork tender. Drain, return it back to the hot pan, and let it stand for 2 to 3 minutes with the lid on.
2. Transfer the cauliflower and garlic to a food processor or blender. Add the olive oil, salt, and pepper, then purée until smooth.
3. Taste and adjust the salt and pepper. Remove to a serving bowl and add the parsley and mix until combined.
4. Garnish with additional olive oil, if desired. Serve immediately.

Nutrition Info per Serving:
Calories: 99, Protein: 4 g, Fat: 4 g, Carbohydrates: 15 g, Fibre: 6 g, Sugar: 6 g, Sodium: 214 mg

Vegetarian Caramelised Onions

PREP TIME: 5 MINUTES, COOK TIME: 15 MINUTES, SERVES: 10

- 2 tbsps. extra virgin olive oil
- 1 tsp. erythritol
- ⅛ tsp. cracked black pepper
- 400 g thinly sliced white onions

1. Pour the oil into a medium saucepan and heat it over medium heat. Add onion, erythritol and pepper. Fry for 5 to 10 minutes, stirring constantly. Once the onion is translucent and begins to brown, cover the pot.
2. Turn to low heat, let the onions "sweat" for another 5 minutes. When finished, they should be dark brown and very soft.

Nutrition Info per Serving:
Calories: 47, Protein: 1 g, Fat: 4 g, Carbohydrates: 3 g, Fibre: 0.5 g, Sugar: 1 g, Sodium: 2 mg

Breaded Artichoke Hearts

⏱ PREP TIME: 5 MINUTES, COOK TIME: 8 MINUTES, SERVES: 14

- 14 whole artichoke hearts, packed in water
- 1 egg
- 60 g almond meal
- 20 g panko bread crumbs
- 1 tsp. Italian seasoning
- Cooking spray

1. Preheat the air fryer to 190ºC.
2. Squeeze excess water from the artichoke hearts and place them on paper towels to dry.
3. In a small bowl, beat the egg. In another small bowl, place the almond meal. In a third small bowl, combine the bread crumbs and Italian seasoning, and stir.
4. Spritz the air fryer basket with cooking spray.
5. Dip the artichoke hearts in the almond meal, then the egg, and then the bread crumb mixture.
6. Place the breaded artichoke hearts in the air fryer. Spray them with cooking spray. Air fry for 8 minutes, or until the artichoke hearts have browned and are crisp, flipping once halfway through.
7. Let cool for 5 minutes before serving.

Nutrition Info per Serving:
Calories: 50, Protein: 2 g, Fat: 3 g, Carbohydrates: 4 g, Fibre: 2 g, Sugar: 0.5 g, Sodium: 123 mg

Roasted Cauliflower with Lemon Zest

⏱ PREP TIME: 5 MINUTES, COOK TIME: 20 MINUTES, SERVES: 4

- 500 g cauliflower florets (1 small head cauliflower)
- 4 tbsps. extra virgin olive oil
- 3 large cloves garlic, minced
- ½ tsp. chilli pepper flakes
- Grated zest of 1 large lemon
- ⅛ tsp. sea salt
- ⅛ tsp. cracked black pepper
- 3 tbsps. chopped fresh basil

1. Preheat the oven to 205°C. Remove and discard the stems and core of the cauliflower. Place the cauliflower head in an 20- by 20-cm baking pan.
2. Drizzle with oil, and then sprinkle on the garlic, chilli pepper flakes, lemon zest, salt, and pepper. Toss generously until the ingredients cover the cauliflower.
3. Bake for 15 to 20 minutes, shaking the pan after 10 minutes to prevent the cauliflower from sticking. Remove from the heat, top with fresh basil, and serve immediately.

Nutrition Info per Serving:
Calories: 163, Protein: 4 g, Fat: 14 g, Carbohydrates: 8 g, Fibre: 3 g, Sugar: 3 g, Sodium: 97 mg

Asian Fried Aubergine

PREP TIME: 10 MINUTES, COOK TIME: 40 MINUTES, SERVES: 4

- 1 large aubergine, sliced into fourths
- 3 spring onions, diced, green tips only
- 1 tsp. fresh ginger, peeled & diced fine
- 30 g ground almonds
- 1 tsp. cornflour
- 1½ tbsps. soy sauce
- 1½ tbsps. sesame oil
- 1 tbsp. vegetable oil
- 1 tbsp. fish sauce
- 2 tsps. erythritol
- ¼ tsp. salt

1. Place aubergine on paper towels and sprinkle both sides with salt. Let for 1 hour to remove excess moisture. Pat dry with more paper towels.
2. In a small bowl, whisk together soy sauce, sesame oil, fish sauce, erythritol, and cornflour.
3. Coat both sides of the aubergine with the ground almonds, use more if needed.
4. Heat oil in a large frying pan, over med-high heat. Add ½ the ginger and 1 spring onion, then lay 2 slices of aubergine on top. Use ½ the sauce mixture to lightly coat both sides of the aubergine. Cook for 8-10 minutes per side. Repeat.
5. Serve garnished with remaining spring onions.

Nutrition Info per Serving:
Calories: 214, Protein: 5 g, Fat: 16 g, Carbohydrates: 14 g, Fibre: 4 g, Sugar: 4 g, Sodium: 726 mg

---

Ratatouille with Herbs

PREP TIME: 10 MINUTES, COOK TIME: 50 MINUTES, SERVES: 4 TO 6

- 2 large onions, cut into 2.5-cm pieces
- 8 large garlic cloves, peeled and smashed
- 80 ml plus 15 ml extra-virgin olive oil
- Salt and pepper
- 700 g aubergine, peeled and cut into 2.5-cm pieces
- 1 kg plum tomatoes, peeled, cored, and chopped coarse
- 2 small courgettes, halved lengthwise and cut into 2.5-cm pieces
- 1½ tsp. herbes de Provence
- ¼ tsp. red pepper flakes
- 1 bay leaf
- 2 tbsps. chopped fresh basil
- 1 tbsp. minced fresh parsley
- 1 tbsp. sherry vinegar
- 1 red pepper, stemmed, seeded, and cut into 2.5-cm pieces
- 1 yellow pepper, stemmed, seeded, and cut into 2.5-cm pieces

1. Put oven rack to middle position and heat oven to 205°C. Heat 80 ml oil in Dutch oven over medium-high heat until shimmering. Add garlic, onions, 1 tsp. salt, and ¼ tsp. pepper and cook for about 10 minutes, stirring occasionally, until onions are translucent and starting to soften. Add herbes de Provence, bay leaf, pepper flakes, and cook for for 1 minute, stirring frequently. Stir in aubergine and tomatoes. Sprinkle with ½ tsp. salt and ¼ tsp. pepper and stir to mix. Transfer pot to oven and cook for 40 to 45 minutes, uncovered, until vegetables are very tender and spotty brown.
2. Remove pot from oven and, using wooden spoon, smash and stir aubergine mixture until broken down to saucelike consistency. Stir in peppers, ¼ tsp. salt, courgettes, and ¼ tsp. pepper and return to oven. Cook for 20 to 25 minutes, uncovered, until courgettes and peppers are just tender.
3. Remove pot from oven, cover, and let sit for 10 to 15 minutes until courgettes are translucent and easily pierced with tip of paring knife. Using wooden spoon, scrape any browned bits from sides of pot and stir back into ratatouille. Discard bay leaf. Stir in 1 tbsp. parsley, basil, and vinegar. Season with salt and pepper. Transfer ratatouille to serving platter, drizzle with 15 ml oil, and sprinkle with basil. Serve.

Nutrition Info per Serving:
Calories: 333, Protein: 5 g, Fat: 24 g, Carbohydrates: 28 g, Fibre: 10 g, Sugar: 14 g, Sodium: 484 mg

Cauliflower Mushroom Risotto

PREP TIME: 10 MINUTES, COOK TIME: 30 MINUTES, SERVES: 2

- 1 medium head cauliflower, grated
- 220 g Porcini mushrooms, sliced
- 1 brown onion, diced fine
- 480 ml low sodium vegetable broth
- 2 tsps. garlic, diced fine
- 2 tsps. white wine vinegar
- Salt & pepper, to taste
- Olive oil cooking spray

1. Heat oven to 180°C. Line a baking sheet with foil.
2. Place the mushrooms on the prepared pan and spray with cooking spray. Sprinkle with salt and toss to coat. Bake for 10-12 minutes, or until golden brown and the mushrooms start to crisp.
3. Spray a large frying pan with cooking spray and place over med-high heat. Add onion and cook, stirring frequently, until translucent, about 3-4 minutes. Add garlic and cook 2 minutes, until golden.
4. Add the cauliflower and cook 1 minute, stirring.
5. Place the broth in a saucepan and bring to a simmer. Add to the frying pan, 60 ml at a time, mixing well after each addition.
6. Stir in vinegar. Reduce heat to low and let simmer, 4-5 minutes, or until most of the liquid has evaporated.
7. Spoon cauliflower mixture onto plates, or in bowls, and top with mushrooms. Serve.

Nutrition Info per Serving:
Calories: 180, Protein: 11 g, Fat: 2 g, Carbohydrates: 37 g, Fibre: 12 g, Sugar: 13 g, Sodium: 408 mg

Grilled Ultimate Portobello Burger

PREP TIME: 10 MINUTES, COOK TIME: 40 MINUTES, SERVES: 4

- 4 tbsps. extra virgin olive oil
- 4 100% wholemeal hamburger buns
- 4 medium portobello mushrooms (about 10-cm in diameter)
- 4 tbsps. prepared pesto
- 4 tbsps. caramelised onions
- ¼ tsp. sea salt
- ½ tsp. ground black pepper
- 8 tbsps. balsamic vinegar

1. Clean the mushrooms by wiping them with a damp towel. Remove the mushroom stems, and then scoop out the brown gills with a metal spoon and discard them.
2. Brush each mushroom top with a tbsp. of oil, and sprinkle the inside of each mushroom with salt, pepper, and 2 tbsps. of balsamic vinegar. Set aside for at least 20 minutes.
3. Place the mushrooms on a hot grill or grill pan, top down. Grill for about 5 to 7 minutes per side, or until tender. Don't handle them too much to prevent the juices from being released.
4. Toast the buns while the mushrooms are grilling by placing them face down on the grill for about 1 minute. Remove from the grill, and spread 1 tbsp. of pesto on the inside of each top bun.
5. Place a mushroom on each bottom bun, then top with 1 tbsp. of caramelised onions.

Nutrition Info per Serving:
Calories: 387, Protein: 10 g, Fat: 20 g, Carbohydrates: 44 g, Fibre: 6 g, Sugar: 8 g, Sodium: 641 mg

Chapter 8: Poultry

Chicken and Spinach Stew

PREP TIME: 13 MINUTES, COOK TIME: 10 MINUTES, SERVES: 6

- 1 ginger, sliced
- 3 garlic cloves, minced
- 60 g spinach leaves
- 180 g chopped tomatoes
- 500 g chicken breasts
- 250 ml water
- Salt and pepper, to taste

1. Press the Sauté button on the Instant Pot and add the chicken and garlic. Stir-fry for 3 minutes until the garlic becomes fragrant.
2. Add the ginger, tomatoes, spinach, and water. Season with salt and pepper.
3. Lock the lid. Select the Manual mode and set the cooking time for 6 minutes at High Pressure.
4. Once cooking is complete, do a natural pressure release for 5 minutes, then release any remaining pressure. Carefully open the lid.
5. Cool for a few minutes and serve warm.

Nutrition Info per Serving:
Calories: 149, Protein: 26 g, Fat: 3 g, Carbohydrates: 5 g, Fibre: 1 g, Sugar: 2 g, Sodium: 89 mg

Barbecue Chicken Wings

PREP TIME: 5 MINUTES, COOK TIME: 12 MINUTES, SERVES: 4

- 500 g chicken wings
- 1 tsp. salt
- ½ tsp. pepper
- ¼ tsp. garlic powder
- 250 ml sugar-free barbecue sauce, divided
- 250 ml water

1. Toss the chicken wings with the salt, pepper, garlic powder, and half of barbecue sauce in a large bowl until well coated.
2. Pour the water into the Instant Pot and insert the trivet. Place the wings on the trivet.
3. Secure the lid. Select the Manual mode and set the cooking time for 12 minutes at High Pressure.
4. Once cooking is complete, do a quick pressure release. Carefully open the lid.
5. Transfer the wings to a serving bowl and toss with the remaining sauce. Serve immediately.

Nutrition Info per Serving:
Calories: 323, Protein: 23 g, Fat: 23 g, Carbohydrates: 8 g, Fibre: 1 g, Sugar: 1 g, Sodium: 836 mg

Chicken and Mushroom Casserole

⏲ PREP TIME: 15 MINUTES, COOK TIME: 20 MINUTES, SERVES: 4

- 4 chicken breasts
- 1 tbsp. curry powder
- 250 ml light coconut milk
- Salt, to taste
- 1 broccoli, cut into florets
- 70 g mushrooms
- 60 g shredded low-fat Parmesan cheese
- Cooking spray

1. Preheat the air fryer to 180ºC. Spritz a casserole dish with cooking spray.
2. Cube the chicken breasts and combine with curry powder and coconut milk in a bowl. Season with salt.
3. Add the broccoli and mushroom and mix well.
4. Pour the mixture into the casserole dish. Top with the cheese.
5. Transfer to the air fryer and bake for about 20 minutes.
6. Serve warm.

Nutrition Info per Serving:
Calories: 324, Protein: 36 g, Fat: 10 g, Carbohydrates: 24 g, Fibre: 6 g, Sugar: 5 g, Sodium: 517 mg

Herbed Turkey Breast

⏲ PREP TIME: 20 MINUTES, COOK TIME: 45 MINUTES, SERVES: 6

- Cooking spray
- 1 tbsp. olive oil
- 2 garlic cloves, minced
- 2 tsps. Dijon mustard
- 1½ tsps. rosemary
- 1½ tsps. sage
- 1½ tsps. thyme
- 1 tsp. salt
- ½ tsp. freshly ground black pepper
- 1.4 kg turkey breast, thawed if frozen

1. Preheat the air fryer to 190ºC. Spray the air fryer basket lightly with cooking spray.
2. In a small bowl, mix together the garlic, olive oil, Dijon mustard, rosemary, sage, thyme, salt, and pepper to make a paste. Smear the paste all over the turkey breast.
3. Place the turkey breast in the air fryer basket. Air fry for 20 minutes. Flip turkey breast over and baste it with any drippings that have collected in the bottom drawer of the air fryer. Air fry until the internal temperature of the meat reaches at least 77ºC, 20 more minutes.
4. If desired, increase the temperature to 205ºC, flip the turkey breast over one last time, and air fry for 5 minutes to get a crispy exterior.
5. Let the turkey rest for 10 minutes before slicing and serving.

Nutrition Info per Serving:
Calories: 256, Protein: 40 g, Fat: 9 g, Carbohydrates: 0 g, Fibre: 0 g, Sugar: 0 g, Sodium: 619 mg

Whole Chicken Roast

⏲ PREP TIME: 10 MINUTES, COOK TIME: 1 HOUR, SERVES: 6

- 1 tsp. salt
- 1 tsp. Italian seasoning
- ½ tsp. freshly ground black pepper
- ½ tsp. paprika
- ½ tsp. garlic powder
- ½ tsp. onion powder
- 2 tbsps. olive oil, plus more as needed
- 1.8-kg fryer chicken

1. Preheat the air fryer to 180ºC.
2. Grease the air fryer basket lightly with olive oil.
3. In a small bowl, mix the salt, Italian seasoning, pepper, paprika, garlic powder, and onion powder.
4. Remove any giblets from the chicken. Pat the chicken dry thoroughly with paper towels, including the cavity.
5. Brush the chicken all over with the olive oil and rub it with the seasoning mixture.
6. Truss the chicken or tie the legs with butcher's twine. This will make it easier to flip the chicken during cooking.
7. Put the chicken in the air fryer basket, breast-side down. Air fry for 30 minutes. Flip the chicken over and baste it with any drippings collected in the bottom drawer of the air fryer. Lightly brush the chicken with olive oil.
8. Air fry for 20 minutes. Flip the chicken over one last time and air fry until a thermometer inserted into the thickest part of the thigh reaches at least 75ºC and it's crispy and golden, 10 more minutes. Continue to cook, checking every 5 minutes until the chicken reaches the correct internal temperature.
9. Let the chicken rest for 10 minutes before carving and serving.

Nutrition Info per Serving:
Calories: 399, Protein: 30 g, Fat: 31 g, Carbohydrates: 1 g, Fibre: 0 g, Sugar: 0 g, Sodium: 457 mg

Turkey Hoisin Burgers

⏲ PREP TIME: 10 MINUTES, COOK TIME: 20 MINUTES, SERVES: 4

- 500 g lean minced turkey
- 15 g panko bread crumbs
- 60 ml hoisin sauce
- 2 tbsps. soy sauce
- 4 wholemeal buns
- Olive oil spray

1. In a large bowl, mix together the turkey, bread crumbs, hoisin sauce, and soy sauce.
2. Form the mixture into 4 equal patties. Cover with clingfilm and refrigerate the patties for 30 minutes.
3. Preheat the air fryer to 190ºC. Spray the air fryer basket lightly with olive oil spray.
4. Place the patties in the air fryer basket in a single layer. Spray the patties lightly with olive oil spray.
5. Air fry for 10 minutes. Flip the patties over, lightly spray with olive oil spray, and air fry for an additional 5 to 10 minutes, until golden brown.
6. Place the patties on buns and top with your choice of low-calorie burger toppings like sliced tomatoes, onions, and cabbage slaw. Serve immediately.

Nutrition Info per Serving:
Calories: 364, Protein: 29 g, Fat: 11 g, Carbohydrates: 39 g, Fibre: 4 g, Sugar: 7 g, Sodium: 781 mg

Chapter 8: Poultry / 39

Chicken Fajita Bowls

⏲ *PREP TIME: 5 MINUTES, COOK TIME: 10 MINUTES, SERVES: 2*

- 500 g boneless, skinless chicken breasts, cut into 2.5-cm pieces
- 500 ml chicken broth
- 250 ml salsa
- 1 tsp. paprika
- 1 tsp. fine sea salt, or more to taste
- 1 tsp. chilli powder
- ½ tsp. ground cumin
- ½ tsp. ground black pepper
- 1 lime, halved

1. Combine all the ingredients except the lime in the Instant Pot.
2. Lock the lid. Select the Manual mode and set the cooking time for 10 minutes at High Pressure.
3. When the timer beeps, perform a quick pressure release. Carefully remove the lid.
4. Shred the chicken with two forks and return to the Instant Pot. Squeeze the lime juice into the chicken mixture. Taste and add more salt, if needed. Give the mixture a good stir.
5. Ladle the chicken mixture into bowls and serve.

Nutrition Info per Serving:
Calories: 412, Protein: 58 g, Fat: 6 g, Carbohydrates: 28 g, Fibre: 5 g, Sugar: 7 g, Sodium: 1024 mg

....

Broccoli Chicken with Black Beans

⏲ *PREP TIME: 10 MINUTES, COOK TIME: 25 MINUTES, SERVES: 4*

- 1 tbsp. olive oil
- 2 chicken breasts, skinless and boneless
- 70 g broccoli florets
- 375 ml chicken stock
- 2 tbsps. tomato sauce
- 200 g black beans, soaked overnight and drained
- A pinch of salt and black pepper

1. Set your Instant Pot to Sauté and heat the olive oil. Add the chicken breasts and sauté for 5 minutes until lightly browned.
2. Add the remaining ingredients to the pot and stir well.
3. Lock the lid. Select the Poultry mode and cook for 20 minutes at High Pressure.
4. Once cooking is complete, do a natural pressure release for 10 minutes, then release any remaining pressure. Carefully open the lid.
5. Remove from the pot and serve on plates.

Nutrition Info per Serving:
Calories: 297, Protein: 34 g, Fat: 8 g, Carbohydrates: 23 g, Fibre: 7 g, Sugar: 2 g, Sodium: 660 mg

Easy Asian Turkey Meatballs

PREP TIME: 10 MINUTES, COOK TIME: 11 TO 14 MINUTES, SERVES: 4

- 2 tbsps. peanut oil, divided
- 1 small onion, minced
- 40 g water chestnuts, finely chopped
- ½ tsp. ground ginger
- 2 tbsps. low-sodium soy sauce
- 25 g panko bread crumbs
- 1 egg, beaten
- 500 g minced turkey

1. Preheat the air fryer to 205°C.
2. In a round metal pan, combine 1 tbsp. of peanut oil and onion. Air fry for 1 to 2 minutes or until crisp and tender. Transfer the onion to a medium bowl.
3. Add the water chestnuts, ground ginger, soy sauce, and bread crumbs to the onion and mix well. Add egg and stir well. Mix in the minced turkey until combined.
4. Form the mixture into 2.5-cm meatballs. Drizzle the remaining 1 tbsp. of oil over the meatballs.
5. Bake the meatballs in the pan in batches for 10 to 12 minutes or until they are 75°C on a meat thermometer. Rest for 5 minutes before serving.

Nutrition Info per Serving:
Calories: 332, Protein: 24 g, Fat: 21 g, Carbohydrates: 13 g, Fibre: 1 g, Sugar: 2 g, Sodium: 472 mg

Chicken Curry

PREP TIME: 6 MINUTES, COOK TIME: 15 MINUTES, SERVES: 6

- 500 ml freshly squeezed coconut milk
- 700 g boneless chicken breasts
- 400 g chopped tomatoes
- 2 tbsps. curry powder
- 1 ginger
- Salt and pepper, to taste

1. Press the Sauté button on the Instant Pot. Add the chicken breasts and cook for 3 minutes until lightly golden. Season with salt and pepper.
2. Stir in the curry powder and continue cooking for 2 minutes more. Add the remaining ingredients and whisk well.
3. Press the Poultry button and set the cooking time for 10 minutes.
4. Once cooking is complete, do a natural pressure release for 6 minutes, then release any remaining pressure. Carefully open the lid.
5. Cool for 5 minutes and serve on plates.

Nutrition Info per Serving:
Calories: 290, Protein: 27 g, Fat: 19 g, Carbohydrates: 7 g, Fibre: 2 g, Sugar: 3 g, Sodium: 198 mg

Chapter 9: Meats

Air Fried Ribeye Steak

⏱ PREP TIME: 5 MINUTES, COOK TIME: 15 MINUTES, SERVES: 1

- 1 (500-g) ribeye steak
- Salt and ground black pepper, to taste
- 1 tbsp. peanut oil
- ½ tbsp. peanut butter
- ½ tsp. thyme, chopped

1. Preheat a frying pan in the air fryer at 205ºC.
2. Season the steak with salt and pepper. Remove the frying pan from the air fryer once preheated.
3. Put the frying pan on the hob on a medium heat and drizzle with the peanut oil.
4. Sear the steak for 2 minutes.
5. Turn over the steak and place in the air fryer for 6 minutes.
6. Take out the steak from the air fryer and place it back on the hob on low heat to keep warm.
7. Toss in the peanut butter and thyme and air fry for 3 minutes.
8. Rest for 5 minutes and serve.

Nutrition Info per Serving:
Calories: 746, Protein: 53 g, Fat: 58 g, Carbohydrates: 1 g, Fibre: 0 g, Sugar: 0 g, Sodium: 90 mg

Braising Steak with Brussels Sprouts

⏱ PREP TIME: 20 MINUTES, COOK TIME: 25 MINUTES, SERVES: 4

- 500 g beef braising steak
- 2 tbsps. olive oil
- 1 tbsp. red wine vinegar
- 1 tsp. fine sea salt
- ½ tsp. ground black pepper
- 1 tsp. smoked paprika
- 1 tsp. onion powder
- ½ tsp. garlic powder
- 230 g Brussels sprouts, cleaned and halved
- ½ tsp. fennel seeds
- 1 tsp. dried basil
- 1 tsp. dried sage

1. Massage the beef with the olive oil, wine vinegar, salt, black pepper, paprika, onion powder, and garlic powder, coating it well.
2. Allow to marinate for a minimum of 3 hours.
3. Preheat the air fryer to 200ºC.
4. Remove the beef from the marinade and put in the preheated air fryer. Air fry for 10 minutes. Flip the beef halfway through.
5. Put the prepared Brussels sprouts in the air fryer along with the fennel seeds, basil, and sage.
6. Lower the heat to 190ºC and air fry everything for another 5 minutes.
7. Give them a good stir. Air fry for an additional 10 minutes.
8. Serve immediately.

Nutrition Info per Serving:
Calories: 465, Protein: 36 g, Fat: 33 g, Carbohydrates: 8 g, Fibre: 3 g, Sugar: 2 g, Sodium: 676 mg

Garlicky Lamb Chops

PREP TIME: 20 MINUTES, COOK TIME: 22 MINUTES, SERVES: 4

- 1 tbsp. fresh oregano, chopped
- 1 tbsp. fresh thyme, chopped
- 8 (110-g) lamb chops
- 60 ml olive oil, divided
- 1 bulb of garlic
- Salt and black pepper, to taste

1. Preheat the Air fryer to 200ºC and grease an Air fryer basket.
2. Rub the garlic bulb with about 2 tbsps. of the olive oil.
3. Arrange the garlic bulb in the Air fryer basket and air fry for about 12 minutes.
4. Mix remaining oil, herbs, salt and black pepper in a large bowl.
5. Coat the lamb chops with about 1 tbsp. of the herb mixture.
6. Place half of the chops in the Air fryer basket with garlic bulb and roast for about 5 minutes.
7. Repeat with the remaining lamb chops and serve with herb mixture.

Nutrition Info per Serving:
Calories: 528, Protein: 35 g, Fat: 41 g, Carbohydrates: 3 g, Fibre: 1 g, Sugar: 0 g, Sodium: 103 mg

Lamb Rack with Pesto Sauce

PREP TIME: 15 MINUTES, COOK TIME: 45 MINUTES, SERVES: 4

- 500 g lamb rack
- 2 tbsps. pesto sauce
- 1 tsp. chilli powder
- 1 tbsp. coconut oil
- 250 ml water

1. Rub the lamb rack with pesto sauce and chilli powder. Let sit for 15 minutes to marinate.
2. Heat the coconut oil in the Instant Pot on Sauté mode for 3 minutes.
3. Put the marinated lamb in the hot oil and cook on Sauté mode for 4 minutes on each side. Pour in the water.
4. Close the lid. Select Manual mode and set cooking time for 45 minutes on High Pressure.
5. When timer beeps, use a quick pressure release. Open the lid.
6. Serve immediately.

Nutrition Info per Serving:
Calories: 430, Protein: 25 g, Fat: 36 g, Carbohydrates: 1 g, Fibre: 0 g, Sugar: 0 g, Sodium: 176 mg

Slow Cooked Lamb Shanks

⏱ PREP TIME: 10 MINUTES, COOK TIME: 55 MINUTES, SERVES: 4

- 2 tbsps. olive oil
- 1 kg lamb shanks
- Salt and black pepper, to taste
- 6 garlic cloves, minced
- 250 ml chicken broth
- 180 ml red wine
- 400 g crushed tomatoes
- 1 tsp. dried oregano
- 5 g chopped parsley, for garnish

❶ Press the Sauté button on the Instant Pot. Heat the olive oil and add the lamb to the pot. Season with salt and pepper. Sear the lamb on both sides for 6 minutes, or until browned. Transfer the lamb to a plate and set aside.
❷ Add the garlic to the pot and sauté for 30 seconds, or until fragrant. Stir in the chicken broth and red wine and cook for 2 minutes, stirring constantly. Add the tomatoes and oregano. Stir and cook for 2 minutes. Return the lamb to the pot and baste with the chicken broth mixture.
❸ Lock the lid. Select the Manual setting and set the cooking time for 45 minutes on High Pressure.
❹ When the timer beeps, do a natural pressure release for 15 minutes, then release any remaining pressure. Open the lid. Top with the chopped parsley and adjust the taste with salt and pepper.
❺ Divide among 4 plates and serve warm.

Nutrition Info per Serving:
Calories: 548, Protein: 33 g, Fat: 38 g, Carbohydrates: 10 g, Fibre: 2 g, Sugar: 5 g, Sodium: 503 mg

Garlic Pork Chops

⏱ PREP TIME: 5 MINUTES, COOK TIME: 10 MINUTES, SERVES: 6

- 6 boneless pork loin chops, trim excess fat
- 60 ml lemon juice
- ¼ tsp. liquid stevia
- 60 ml low sodium soy sauce
- 60 ml dry white wine
- 2 tbsps. garlic, diced fine
- 1 tbsp. vegetable oil
- ¼ tsp. black pepper

❶ Combine lemon juice, liquid stevia, soy sauce, wine, garlic, and pepper in a 23x33-cm baking dish. Mix well.
❷ Add pork chops, turning to coat. Cover and refrigerate at least 4 hours, or overnight, turning chops occasionally.
❸ Heat oil in a large frying pan over med-high heat. Add chops and cook for 2-3 minutes per side.
❹ Pour marinade over chops and bring to a boil. Reduce heat to low and simmer for 2-3 minutes, or chops are desired doneness. Serve topped with sauce.

Nutrition Info per Serving:
Calories: 196, Protein: 21 g, Fat: 10 g, Carbohydrates: 3 g, Fibre: 0 g, Sugar: 0 g, Sodium: 748 mg

Crumbed Golden Fillet Steak

⏱ PREP TIME: 15 MINUTES, COOK TIME: 12 MINUTES, SERVES: 2

- 500 g fillet steak
- Sea salt and ground black pepper, to taste
- ½ tsp. cayenne pepper
- 1 tsp. dried basil
- 1 tsp. dried rosemary
- 1 tsp. dried thyme
- 1 tbsp. sesame oil
- 1 small egg, whisked
- 25 g panko bread crumbs

1. Preheat the air fryer to 180ºC.
2. Cover the fillet steak with the salt, black pepper, cayenne pepper, basil, rosemary, and thyme. Coat with sesame oil.
3. Put the egg in a shallow plate.
4. Pour the bread crumbs in another plate.
5. Dip the fillet steak into the egg. Roll it into the crumbs.
6. Transfer the steak to the air fryer and air fry for 12 minutes or until it turns golden.
7. Serve immediately.

Nutrition Info per Serving:
Calories: 627, Protein: 59 g, Fat: 35 g, Carbohydrates: 14 g, Fibre: 1 g, Sugar: 1 g, Sodium: 330 mg

Crock Pot Carnitas

⏱ PREP TIME: 10 MINUTES, COOK TIME: 6 HOURS, SERVES: 4

- 1.8-kg pork butt, boneless, trim the fat and cut into 5-cm cubes
- 1 onion, cut in half
- Juice from 1 orange, reserve orange halves
- 2 tbsps. fresh lime juice
- 500 ml water
- 1½ tsps. salt
- 1 tsp. cumin
- 1 tsp. oregano
- 2 bay leaves
- ¾ tsp. ground pepper

1. Place pork and orange halves in the crockpot. In a medium bowl, combine remaining ingredients and stir to combine. Pour over pork.
2. Cover and cook on high 5 hours. Pork should be tender enough to shred with a fork. If not, cook another 60 minutes.
3. Transfer pork to a bowl. Pour the sauce into a large saucepan and discard the bay leaves and orange halves.
4. Bring to a boil and cook until it thickens and resembles a syrup.
5. Use two forks to shred the pork. Add pork to the sauce and stir to coat. Serve.

Nutrition Info per Serving:
Calories: 720, Protein: 51 g, Fat: 54 g, Carbohydrates: 11 g, Fibre: 2 g, Sugar: 4 g, Sodium: 812 mg

Nut Crusted Rack of Lamb

⏱ PREP TIME: 15 MINUTES, COOK TIME: 35 MINUTES, SERVES: 6

- 800 g rack of lamb
- 1 egg
- 1 tbsp. breadcrumbs
- 100 g almonds, chopped finely
- 1 tbsp. fresh rosemary, chopped
- 1 tbsp. olive oil
- 1 garlic clove, minced
- Salt and black pepper, to taste

1. Preheat the Air fryer to 105ºC and grease an Air fryer basket.
2. Mix garlic, olive oil, salt and black pepper in a bowl.
3. Whisk the egg in a shallow dish and mix breadcrumbs, almonds and rosemary in another shallow dish.
4. Coat the rack of lamb with garlic mixture evenly, dip into the egg and dredge into the breadcrumb mixture.
5. Arrange the rack of lamb in the Air fryer basket and air fry for about 30 minutes.
6. Set the Air fryer to 200ºC and roast for about 5 more minutes.
7. Dish out and serve warm.

Nutrition Info per Serving:
Calories: 411, Protein: 27 g, Fat: 33 g, Carbohydrates: 5 g, Fibre: 3 g, Sugar: 1 g, Sodium: 92 mg

---

Cajun Smothered Pork Chops

⏱ PREP TIME: 5 MINUTES, COOK TIME: 25 MINUTES, SERVES: 4

- 4 pork chops, thick-cut
- 1 small onion, diced fine
- 70 g mushrooms, sliced
- 250 ml fat free sour cream
- 2 tbsps. almond butter
- 250 ml low sodium chicken broth
- 3 cloves garlic, diced fine
- 1 tbsp. Cajun seasoning
- 2 bay leaves
- 1 tsp. smoked paprika
- Salt & pepper to taste

1. Melt almond butter in a large frying pan over medium heat. Sprinkle chops with salt and pepper and cook until nicely browned, about 5 minutes per side. Transfer to a plate.
2. Add onions and mushrooms and cook until soft, about 5 minutes. Add garlic and cook one minute more.
3. Add broth and stir to incorporate brown bits on bottom of the pan. Add a dash of salt and the bay leaves. Add pork chops back to sauce. Bring to a simmer, cover, and reduce heat. Cook for 5-8 minutes, or until chops are cooked through.
4. Transfer chops to a plate and keep warm. Bring sauce to a boil and cook until it has reduced by half, stirring occasionally.
5. Reduce heat to low and whisk in sour cream, Cajun seasoning, and paprika. Cook, stirring frequently, 3 minutes. Add chops back to the sauce and heat through. Serve.

Nutrition Info per Serving:
Calories: 385, Protein: 38 g, Fat: 22 g, Carbohydrates: 10 g, Fibre: 2 g, Sugar: 3 g, Sodium: 343 mg

Chapter 10: Salads

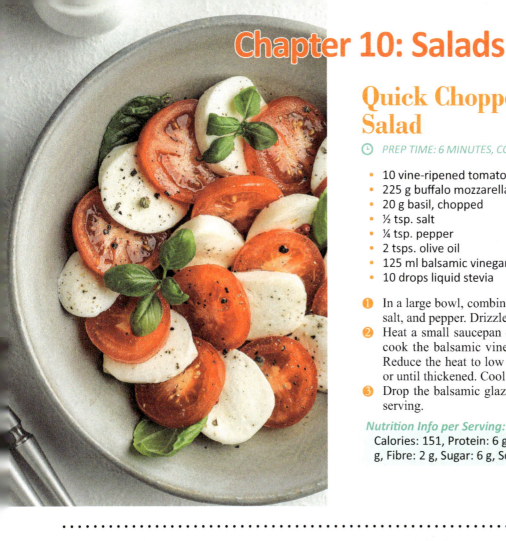

Quick Chopped Caprese Salad

🕒 PREP TIME: 6 MINUTES, COOK TIME: 10 MINUTES, SERVES: 8

- 10 vine-ripened tomatoes, chopped
- 225 g buffalo mozzarella, chopped
- 20 g basil, chopped
- ½ tsp. salt
- ¼ tsp. pepper
- 2 tsps. olive oil
- 125 ml balsamic vinegar
- 10 drops liquid stevia

1. In a large bowl, combine the tomatoes, mozzarella, basil, salt, and pepper. Drizzle with the olive oil.
2. Heat a small saucepan over medium-high heat, add and cook the balsamic vinegar and stevia until simmering. Reduce the heat to low and simmer for 5 to 10 minutes, or until thickened. Cool for 5 minutes.
3. Drop the balsamic glaze over the salad and chill before serving.

Nutrition Info per Serving:
Calories: 151, Protein: 6 g, Fat: 10 g, Carbohydrates: 10 g, Fibre: 2 g, Sugar: 6 g, Sodium: 291 mg

Avocado Cucumber Feta Salad

🕒 PREP TIME: 4 MINUTES, COOK TIME: 0 MINUTES, SERVES: 4

- 2 avocados, chopped
- 2 English cucumbers, chopped
- 120 g low-fat feta cheese, crumbled
- 1 tbsp. olive oil
- 2 tbsps. lemon juice
- ½ tsp. salt
- ¼ tsp. pepper
- Pinch red pepper flakes (optional)

1. In a large bowl, mix all of the ingredients. Chill until ready to enjoy.

Nutrition Info per Serving:
Calories: 307, Protein: 8 g, Fat: 25 g, Carbohydrates: 19 g, Fibre: 10 g, Sugar: 4 g, Sodium: 602 mg

Classic Carrot Apple Salad

PREP TIME: 7 MINUTES, COOK TIME: 1 MINUTE (SIT FOR 30 MINUTES), SERVES: 4

- 2 large Granny Smith apples, cut into matchsticks (about 180 g)
- 2 large carrots, cut into matchsticks (about 150 g)
- 250 ml unsweetened coconut yoghurt
- 40 g sultanas
- 1 tsp. ground cinnamon
- ¼ tsp. ground ginger
- ¼ tsp. curry powder

1. In a medium bowl, mix the apples and carrots into the yoghurt, and then stir in the remaining ingredients.
2. Let sit for at least 30 minutes before serving.

Nutrition Info per Serving:
Calories: 163, Protein: 2 g, Fat: 5 g, Carbohydrates: 31 g, Fibre: 5 g, Sugar: 20 g, Sodium: 27 mg

Caprese Salad Quinoa Bowl

PREP TIME: 10 MINUTES, COOK TIME: 0 MINUTES, SERVES: 2

- 200 g cooked quinoa, cooled completely
- 120 g baby spinach
- 40 g fresh basil, roughly chopped
- 2 tbsps. extra-virgin olive oil
- 1 tbsp. lemon juice, freshly squeezed
- 200 g cherry tomatoes, diced
- 170 g fresh mozzarella, diced
- 1 tsp. balsamic glaze

1. In a large bowl, place the spinach and basil.
2. In a small bowl, whisk the oil and lemon juice to combine. Portion the dressing evenly into 2 stainless-steel salad dressing containers.
3. Evenly divide the greens into 2 large glass meal-prep containers with lids. Top with the cooked quinoa, diced tomatoes, and mozzarella. Drizzle each with ½ tsp. of balsamic glaze. Cover and refrigerate.

Nutrition Info per Serving:
Calories: 580, Protein: 24 g, Fat: 35 g, Carbohydrates: 47 g, Fibre: 7 g, Sugar: 5 g, Sodium: 386 mg

Lemon Avocado Tuna Salad

PREP TIME: 7 MINUTES, COOK TIME: 0 MINUTES, SERVES: 4

- 1 tbsp. extra-virgin olive oil
- 1 avocado, peeled, pitted, and diced
- 2 (170-g) cans albacore tuna, drained
- 20 g thinly sliced red onion
- Juice and zest of 1 lemon
- 1 tsp. sea salt
- ½ tsp. freshly ground black pepper

1. In a medium bowl, add the tuna and break it into chunks with a fork.
2. Place the olive oil, diced avocado, red onion, lemon juice and zest, salt, and pepper. Toss gently.
3. Serve right away over greens, or store in a covered container in the refrigerator for 1 to 2 days.

Nutrition Info per Serving:
Calories: 258, Protein: 24 g, Fat: 16 g, Carbohydrates: 7 g, Fibre: 5 g, Sugar: 1 g, Sodium: 686 mg

----

Chickpea Salad with Olives and Cucumber

PREP TIME: 13 MINUTES, COOK TIME: 0 MINUTES, SERVES: 4

For the Dressing:
- 80 ml extra-virgin olive oil
- 2½ tbsps. freshly squeezed lemon juice
- 2 drops liquid stevia
- 1 tsp. Dijon mustard
- Sea salt
- Freshly ground black pepper

For the Salad:
- 1 (450-g) can chickpeas, drained and rinsed
- 120 g baby rocket
- 150 g Kalamata olives, sliced
- 150 g diced English cucumber
- 200 g cherry tomatoes, halved
- 50 g low-fat feta cheese

Make the Dressing:
1. In a small bowl, whisk the olive oil, lemon juice, stevia, Dijon mustard, salt, and pepper until well combined. Alternatively, pour in a small Mason jar, seal, and shake vigorously until well combined. Keep aside.

Make the Salad:
2. Distribute the chickpeas, rocket, tomatoes, cucumber, olives, and feta equally among 4 bowls.
3. Top each bowl with 1 to 2 tbsps. of dressing and serve.

Nutrition Info per Serving:
Calories: 192, Protein: 14 g, Fat: 8 g, Carbohydrates: 18 g, Fibre: 3 g, Sugar: 0.1 g, Sodium: 160 mg

Asparagus Salad

⏱ *PREP TIME: 22 MINUTES, COOK TIME: 0 MINUTES, SERVES: 6*

- 3 bunches fresh asparagus (about 30 spears)
- 1 tbsp. olive oil
- 1 small red onion, peeled and thinly sliced
- 2 tbsps. fresh orange juice
- 2 tbsps. fresh lemon juice
- 60 g pecans, chopped
- 50 g shaved low-fat Parmesan cheese
- 2 tbsps. fresh thyme, chopped
- Black pepper, freshly ground

1. Trim the woody ends off the asparagus.
2. Lay an asparagus stalk on a cutting board and shave off long ribbons with a peeler until the stalk is used up. Repeat with all the spears.
3. In a large bowl, coat the asparagus ribbons with the olive oil.
4. Add the onion, orange juice, and lemon juice and toss to combine.
5. Add the pecans, Parmesan cheese, and thyme.
6. Season with pepper.
7. Serve immediately or store the salad in an airtight container in the refrigerator for up to 6 hours.

Nutrition Info per Serving:
Calories: 115, Protein: 6 g, Fat: 8 g, Carbohydrates: 8 g, Fibre: 4 g, Sugar: 3 g, Sodium: 82 mg

Cherry Tomato and Avocado Salad

⏱ *PREP TIME: 9 MINUTES, COOK TIME: 0 MINUTES, SERVES: 4*

- 350 g multi-coloured cherry or grape tomatoes
- 1 large ripe avocado, peeled and pitted
- 20 g very thinly sliced red onion
- 30 g low-fat feta cheese, crumbled
- 1 to 2 tbsps. freshly squeezed lime juice (juice of ½ lime)
- 1 tbsp. chopped fresh coriander
- ¼ tsp. coarse salt

1. Chop the tomatoes and avocado into equal bite-size pieces and place in a large bowl.
2. Put the onion, cheese, lime juice, coriander, and salt and toss to combine well. Serve right away.

Nutrition Info per Serving:
Calories: 150, Protein: 3 g, Fat: 11 g, Carbohydrates: 12 g, Fibre: 6 g, Sugar: 3 g, Sodium: 173 mg

Tuscan Tuna and Bean Salad

⏱ *PREP TIME: 6 MINUTES, COOK TIME: 0 MINUTES, SERVES: 4*

- 1 (425-g) can white kidney beans, drained and rinsed
- 2 (150-g) cans tuna packed in oil
- 120 g baby spinach
- 1 tomato, diced
- 1 avocado, pitted and cubed
- ½ small red onion, sliced
- Zest of 1 lemon
- Juice of 1 lemon
- Sea salt
- Freshly ground black pepper

1. Add all the ingredients in a large bowl. Gently toss the ingredients together with two wooden spoons, ensuring they are mixed together evenly.
2. Divide the salad equally among 4 bowls. Serve right away.

Nutrition Info per Serving:
Calories: 414, Protein: 35 g, Fat: 18 g, Carbohydrates: 29 g, Fibre: 12 g, Sugar: 2 g, Sodium: 468 mg

Roasted Beetroot and Pistachio Salad

⏱ *PREP TIME: 5 MINUTES, COOK TIME: 30 MINUTES, SERVES: 4*

- 3 tbsps. extra-virgin olive oil, divided
- 4 medium beetroots, quartered
- 30 g pistachios, chopped
- 30 g low-fat goat's cheese, crumbled
- 2 tbsps. rice vinegar
- ¼ tsp. pink salt

1. Preheat the oven to 205ºC.
2. Mix 2 tbsps. of olive oil with the rice vinegar and salt in a bowl. Keep aside.
3. Line a baking sheet with parchment paper. Gently toss the beetroots with the remaining tbsp. of olive oil and place on the baking sheet.
4. Cover with another sheet of parchment paper and bake for 25 to 30 minutes, until the beetroots are tender.
5. Allow the beetroots to cool and take them to a bowl.
6. Toss the beetroots in the olive oil dressing and transfer to a serving plate.
7. Put goat's cheese and pistachios on top. Enjoy!

Nutrition Info per Serving:
Calories: 258, Protein: 7 g, Fat: 20 g, Carbohydrates: 15 g, Fibre: 4 g, Sugar: 8 g, Sodium: 261 mg

Chapter 11: Soup and Stew

Calamari Stew

⏱ PREP TIME: 12 MINUTES, COOK TIME: 32 MINUTES, SERVES: 3

- 1 tbsp. olive oil
- 500 g separated calamari
- 60 ml white wine
- ½ bunch parsley, chopped
- 200 g tomatoes, chopped

1. Set the Instant Pot to Sauté and add the oil and calamari. Stir to combine well.
2. Lock the lid. Select the Manual mode, then set the timer for 9 minutes at Low Pressure.
3. Once the timer goes off, do a quick pressure release. Carefully open the lid.
4. Add the wine, tomatoes and half of the parsley, and stir well.
5. Lock the lid. Select the Manual mode, then set the timer for 25 minutes at High Pressure.
6. Once the timer goes off, do a quick pressure release. Carefully open the lid.
7. Sprinkle the remaining parsley on top. Divide the soup into bowls and serve.

Nutrition Info per Serving:
Calories: 284, Protein: 32 g, Fat: 7 g, Carbohydrates: 13 g, Fibre: 3 g, Sugar: 6 g, Sodium: 446 mg

Carrot and Bean Chilli

⏱ PREP TIME: 10 MINUTES, COOK TIME: 41 MINUTES, SERVES: 4

- 1 tbsp. olive oil
- 1 small red onion, peeled and diced
- 1 medium green pepper, deseeded and diced
- 1 large carrot, peeled and diced
- 4 cloves garlic, peeled and minced
- 1 small jalapeño, deseeded and diced
- 1 800-g) can diced tomatoes, undrained
- 1 (400-g) can cannellini beans, drained and rinsed
- 1 (400-g) can kidney beans, drained and rinsed
- 1 (400-g) can black beans, drained and rinsed
- 2 tbsps. chilli powder
- 1 tsp. ground cumin
- 1 tsp. salt
- 60 ml vegetable broth

1. Press the Sauté button on the Instant Pot and heat the oil. Add the onion, green pepper and carrot to the pot and sauté for 5 minutes, or until the onion is translucent. Add the garlic and sauté for 1 minute.
2. Stir in the remaining ingredients.
3. Set the lid in place. Select the Meat/Stew setting and set the cooking time for 35 minutes on High Pressure. When the timer goes off, perform a natural pressure release for 15 minutes, then release any remaining pressure. Open the lid.
4. Ladle the chilli into 4 bowls and serve warm.

Nutrition Info per Serving:
Calories: 371, Protein: 15 g, Fat: 5 g, Carbohydrates: 68 g, Fibre: 20 g, Sugar: 9 g, Sodium: 1118 mg

Spinach and Beef Stew

⏲ PREP TIME: 20 MINUTES, COOK TIME: 30 MINUTES, SERVES: 4

- 500 g beef sirloin, chopped
- 60 g spinach, chopped
- 750 ml chicken broth
- 250 ml light coconut milk
- 1 tsp. allspices
- 1 tsp. coconut aminos

1. Put all ingredients in the Instant Pot. Stir to mix well.
2. Close the lid. Set the Manual mode and set cooking time for 30 minutes on High Pressure.
3. When timer beeps, use a natural pressure release for 10 minutes, then release any remaining pressure. Open the lid.
4. Blend with an immersion blender until smooth.
5. Serve warm.

Nutrition Info per Serving:
Calories: 345, Protein: 32 g, Fat: 21 g, Carbohydrates: 7 g, Fibre: 2 g, Sugar: 2 g, Sodium: 718 mg

Tomato and Bean Stew

⏲ PREP TIME: 12 MINUTES, COOK TIME: 20 MINUTES, SERVES: 4

- 1 tbsp. olive oil
- 1 large onion, chopped
- 2 large tomatoes, roughly chopped
- 500 g green beans
- 500 ml low-sodium chicken stock
- Salt and pepper, to taste
- 20 g low-fat Parmesan cheese

1. Press the Sauté bottom on the Instant Pot.
2. Add and heat the olive oil.
3. Add the onions and sauté for 2 minutes until translucent and softened.
4. Add the tomatoes and sauté for 3 to 4 minutes or until soft.
5. Add the beans and stock. Sprinkle with salt and pepper.
6. Lock the lid. Press Manual. Set the timer to 15 minutes at High Pressure.
7. Once the timer goes off, press Cancel. Do a quick pressure release.
8. Open the lid, transfer them in a large bowl and serve with Parmesan cheese on top.

Nutrition Info per Serving:
Calories: 149, Protein: 7 g, Fat: 6 g, Carbohydrates: 19 g, Fibre: 6 g, Sugar: 7 g, Sodium: 278 mg

Chapter 11: Soup and Stew

Delicious Roasted Beetroot Soup

⏱ PREP TIME: 12 MINUTES, COOK TIME: 35 MINUTES, SERVES: 4

- 8 medium beetroots, peeled and cut in quarters
- ½ small sweet onion, peeled and cut into chunks
- 2 garlic cloves, peeled
- 1 tbsp. olive oil
- 2 tbsps. apple cider vinegar
- 500 ml almond milk
- 5 g fresh parsley, chopped

1. Preheat the oven to 180°C. Line a baking sheet with foil.
2. On the baking sheet, arrange the beetroots, onion, and garlic and drizzle the vegetables with the oil.
3. Bake until the beetroots are fork tender, about 35 minutes.
4. In a food processor or blender, combine the vegetables, including any juices on the baking sheet, with the vinegar and almond milk, and process until very smooth.
5. Serve warm, topped with parsley.

Nutrition Info per Serving:
Calories: 147, Protein: 3 g, Fat: 5 g, Carbohydrates: 25 g, Fibre: 6 g, Sugar: 16 g, Sodium: 192 mg

Beef Tomato Stew

⏱ PREP TIME: 12 MINUTES, COOK TIME: 30 MINUTES, SERVES: 4

- 2 tsps. olive oil
- 500 g lean stewing beef
- 400 g diced tomatoes
- 2 spring onions, chopped
- 1 L low-sodium beef broth
- Salt and pepper, to taste

1. Press the Sauté bottom on the Instant Pot.
2. Add and heat the olive oil.
3. Add the meat and sauté for 3 to 4 minutes to evenly brown.
4. Add the tomatoes and onions, then sauté for 3 to 4 minutes or until soft.
5. Pour in the broth. Sprinkle with salt and pepper.
6. Lock the lid. Press Meat/Stew bottom. Set the timer to 20 minutes at High Pressure.
7. Once the timer goes off, press Cancel. Do a quick pressure release.
8. Open the lid, transfer them in a large bowl and serve.

Nutrition Info per Serving:
Calories: 281, Protein: 32 g, Fat: 11 g, Carbohydrates: 12 g, Fibre: 3 g, Sugar: 5 g, Sodium: 546 mg

Chapter 11: Soup and Stew /53

Creamy Vegetable Soup

PREP TIME: 15 MINUTES, COOK TIME: 40 MINUTES, SERVES: 6

1 tsp. olive oil
30 g sweet onion, chopped
2 celery sticks, diced
1 tsp. garlic, minced
1 L fat-free, low-sodium vegetable stock
240 g cauliflower florets, chopped
100 g broccoli florets, chopped
30 g spinach, shredded
230 g silken tofu
1 tsp. white wine vinegar
½ tsp. nutmeg, ground
Black pepper, freshly ground

1. In a large pot over medium heat, heat the oil and sauté the onion, celery, and garlic until softened, about 3 minutes. Add the stock and bring to a boil.
2. Add the cauliflower and broccoli and lower the heat so the soup simmers.
3. Cover the pot and cook until the vegetables are tender, about 25 minutes.
4. Add the spinach and simmer an additional 3 minutes.
5. Transfer the soup to a food processor or blender and purée until it is smooth.
6. Add the tofu and vinegar and purée until silky and smooth.
7. Season with the nutmeg and pepper to taste.
8. Serve warm.

Nutrition Info per Serving:
Calories: 92, Protein: 8 g, Fat: 3 g, Carbohydrates: 12 g, Fibre: 4 g, Sugar: 4 g, Sodium: 163 mg

....

Tomato Chicken Soup

PREP TIME: 6 MINUTES, COOK TIME: 20 MINUTES, SERVES: 4

5 g fresh basil leaves
8 chopped plum tomatoes
4 skinless chicken breasts, halved
Salt and pepper, to taste
1.2 L water

1. Place all ingredients into the Instant Pot. Give a good stir to mix everything.
2. Lock the lid. Select the Manual mode and set the timer to 20 minutes at High Pressure.
3. Once cooking is complete, do a natural pressure release for 10 minutes, then release any remaining pressure. Carefully open the lid.
4. Let the soup cool for 10 minutes and serve warm.

Nutrition Info per Serving:
Calories: 182, Protein: 32 g, Fat: 3 g, Carbohydrates: 8 g, Fibre: 2 g, Sugar: 5 g, Sodium: 187 mg

Mushroom and Beef Chilli

PREP TIME: 15 MINUTES, COOK TIME: 40 MINUTES, SERVES: 6

1 tbsp. olive oil
500 g stewing beef
1 medium onion, peeled and diced
4 cloves garlic, minced
125 ml beef broth
1 (450-g) can chilli beans, undrained
1 (400-g) can diced tomatoes, undrained
150 g sliced mushrooms
2 tbsps. tomato purée
2 tbsps. chilli powder
1 tbsp. Italian seasoning
1 tsp. red pepper flakes
1 tsp. sea salt
½ tsp. ground black pepper

1. Press the Sauté button on the Instant Pot and heat the oil. Add the beef and onion to the pot and sauté for 3 minutes, or until the beef is lightly browned and the onion is translucent. Add the garlic to the pot and sauté for 2 minutes.
2. Pour in the beef broth and deglaze by scraping any of the bits from the bottom and sides of the pot. Stir in the remaining ingredients.
3. Set the lid in place. Select the Meat/Stew setting and set the cooking time for 35 minutes on High Pressure. Once cooking is complete, do a natural pressure release for 15 minutes, then release any remaining pressure. Open the lid.
4. Ladle the chilli into individual bowls and serve warm.

Nutrition Info per Serving:
Calories: 369, Protein: 27 g, Fat: 18 g, Carbohydrates: 26 g, Fibre: 8 g, Sugar: 6 g, Sodium: 943 mg

....

Quick Lentil Bisque

PREP TIME: 2 MINUTES, COOK TIME: 20 MINUTES, SERVES: 2 TO 4

200 g red lentils, washed and drained
1 brown onion, chopped
2 garlic cloves, minced
1 L water
¾ tsp. pink salt
¼ tsp. freshly ground black pepper
1½ tsps. cumin (optional)

1. Combine the lentils, onion, garlic, salt, cumin (if using), and water in a medium stockpot.
2. Bring to a boil, cover, reduce the heat to low and simmer for 20 minutes.
3. Serve right away with freshly ground black pepper, or blend it for a smoother texture.

Nutrition Info per Serving:
Calories: 210, Protein: 14 g, Fat: 1 g, Carbohydrates: 39 g, Fibre: 8 g, Sugar: 2 g, Sodium: 565 mg

Chapter 12: Starter and Sides

Artichoke-Spinach Dip

⏱ PREP TIME: 10 MINUTES, COOK TIME: 10 MINUTES, SERVES: 6-8

- 1 (400-g) can artichoke hearts packed in water, drained and chopped
- 1 (300-g) package frozen spinach, thawed and drained
- 1 tsp. minced garlic
- 2 tbsps. mayonnaise
- 60 ml nonfat plain Greek yoghurt
- 30 g shredded part-skim Mozzarella cheese
- 20 g grated low-fat Parmesan cheese
- ¼ tsp. freshly ground black pepper
- Cooking spray

1. Preheat the air fryer to 180ºC.
2. Wrap the artichoke hearts and spinach in a paper towel and squeeze out any excess liquid, then transfer the vegetables to a large bowl.
3. Add the minced garlic, mayonnaise, plain Greek yoghurt, Mozzarella, Parmesan, and black pepper to the large bowl, stirring well to combine.
4. Spray a baking pan with cooking spray, then transfer the dip mixture to the pan and air fry for 10 minutes.
5. Remove the dip from the air fryer and allow to cool in the pan on a wire rack for 10 minutes before serving.

Nutrition Info per Serving:
Calories: 94, Protein: 5 g, Fat: 7 g, Carbohydrates: 4 g, Fibre: 2 g, Sugar: 0 g, Sodium: 213 mg

Red Peppers and Anchovy Antipasto

⏱ PREP TIME: 5 MINUTES, COOK TIME: 20 MINUTES, SERVES: 4

- 4 red peppers
- 170 g anchovies in oil, chopped
- 150 g Kalamata olives, pitted
- 120 ml olive oil
- Sea salt and freshly ground pepper
- 1 small shallot
- 2 tbsps. capers, rinsed and drained

1. Heat the grill to medium-high heat.
2. Put the red peppers on the grill and cook, flipping frequently, until the skins are charred.
3. Place the peppers in a paper bag and set aside for 10 minutes.
4. When the peppers have cooled down, peel the skins off under cold water, then pat dry with paper towels.
5. Mix the capers, anchovies, olives, shallot, and olive oil in a large bowl.
6. Cut the peppers and toss with the anchovy mixture. Season to taste.
7. Serve with water crackers or crusty bread.

Nutrition Info per Serving:
Calories: 324, Protein: 8 g, Fat: 31 g, Carbohydrates: 10 g, Fibre: 4 g, Sugar: 5 g, Sodium: 920 mg

Baba Ghanoush

PREP TIME: 10 MINUTES, COOK TIME: 20 MINUTES, SERVES: 4

- 2 to 4 garlic cloves, peeled and minced
- 900 g Japanese aubergines
- 1 tbsp. olive oil
- 2 tbsps. lemon juice
- 60 ml tahini

1. Preheat broiler. Put oven rack at least 15-cm from heat source.
2. Cut aubergines in half lengthwise, and place on a lined baking sheet. Brush aubergines with olive oil. Broil aubergines for 15 to 20 minutes, rotating pan once during cooking. Set aside to cool down.
3. When aubergines are cool, scrape the inner flesh from the skins and transfer to a food processor. Discard skins. Add tahini, garlic and lemon juice to food processor. Pulse about 1 minute until smooth, scraping down the sides of the bowl if needed. Serve or refrigerate.

Nutrition Info per Serving:
Calories: 153, Protein: 3 g, Fat: 10 g, Carbohydrates: 15 g, Fibre: 7 g, Sugar: 6 g, Sodium: 11 mg

Tzatziki Greek Yoghurt Dip

PREP TIME: 5 MINUTES, COOK TIME: 3 MINUTES (SIT FOR 30 MINUTES), SERVES: 8

- 430 ml low-fat plain Greek yoghurt
- 1 tbsp. extra virgin olive oil
- 2 large cloves garlic, very finely chopped
- 30 g finely diced English cucumber
- 10 g chopped fresh mint leaves
- Juice of ½ lemon
- ¼ tsp. cracked black pepper
- ⅛ tsp. sea salt

1. Mix well all the chopped ingredients in a large bowl with the yoghurt, lemon juice, and oil. Then add the salt and pepper.
2. Before serving, let the mixture sit for about 30 minutes to an hour so the flavours can meld.

Nutrition Info per Serving:
Calories: 51, Protein: 7 g, Fat: 3 g, Carbohydrates: 3 g, Fibre: 0 g, Sugar: 2 g, Sodium: 53 mg

Healthy Grilled Asparagus

PREP TIME: 10 MINUTES, COOK TIME: 3 MINUTES, SERVES: 4

- 5 tbsps. extra virgin olive oil
- 500 g asparagus
- Grated zest of 1 large lemon
- Juice of ½ lemon
- 3 large cloves garlic, minced
- ¼ tsp. sea salt
- ⅛ tsp. cracked black pepper

1. Cut off and discard the fibrous thick ends of the asparagus spears.
2. In a large baking dish, lay the spears in a single, even layer, and drizzle with oil. Roll the spears in the oil to coat evenly.
3. Add the lemon zest, lemon juice, garlic, salt, and pepper over the top. Roll the spears again to coat all sides with the seasonings.
4. Place on a hot grill, and rotate the spears constantly so they do not burn.
5. Grill for about 2 minutes or to desired tenderness, and then return to marinating pan to serve.

Nutrition Info per Serving:
Calories: 174, Protein: 4 g, Fat: 15 g, Carbohydrates: 9 g, Fibre: 4 g, Sugar: 3 g, Sodium: 153 mg

Air Fried Olives

PREP TIME: 5 MINUTES, COOK TIME: 8 MINUTES, SERVES: 4

- 1 (150-g) jar pitted green olives
- 60 g coconut flour
- Salt and pepper, to taste
- 25 g panko bread crumbs
- 1 egg
- Cooking spray

1. Preheat the air fryer to 205ºC.
2. Remove the olives from the jar and dry thoroughly with paper towels.
3. In a small bowl, combine the flour with salt and pepper to taste. Place the bread crumbs in another small bowl. In a third small bowl, beat the egg.
4. Spritz the air fryer basket with cooking spray.
5. Dip the olives in the flour, then the egg, and then the bread crumbs.
6. Place the breaded olives in the air fryer. It is okay to stack them. Spray the olives with cooking spray. Air fry for 6 minutes. Flip the olives and air fry for an additional 2 minutes, or until brown and crisp.
7. Cool before serving.

Nutrition Info per Serving:
Calories: 165, Protein: 4 g, Fat: 12 g, Carbohydrates: 11 g, Fibre: 4 g, Sugar: 0 g, Sodium: 845 mg

Simple Grilled Prawn

PREP TIME: 5 MINUTES, COOK TIME: 5 MINUTES, SERVES: 10

- 30 prawns, peeled, deveined, and tails left on
- 2 tbsps. olive oil
- 1 tbsp. chilli powder
- 5 drops liquid stevia
- ¼ tsp. freshly ground pepper

1. Preheat a grill to medium-high heat. Soak ten wooden skewers in water.
2. Mix the olive oil, chilli powder, stevia, and pepper in a medium bowl. Put in the prawns and toss to coat.
3. Thread each skewer with 3 prawns.
4. Cook for about 2 minutes per side on the grill, until the prawns are pink. Serve.

Nutrition Info per Serving:
Calories: 70, Protein: 9 g, Fat: 4 g, Carbohydrates: 1 g, Fibre: 0 g, Sugar: 0 g, Sodium: 90 mg

----

Classic Bruschetta

PREP TIME: 10 MINUTES, COOK TIME: 50 MINUTES, SERVES: 8

- 1 large wholemeal baguette (about 32 slices)
- 5 large heirloom tomatoes of various colours, cored and chopped finely
- 20 g finely chopped fresh Italian basil
- 8–10 fresh mint leaves, finely chopped
- 2 large cloves garlic, finely minced
- 60 g finely minced red onion
- 60 ml extra virgin olive oil
- 80 ml balsamic vinegar
- ¼ tsp. sea salt
- ¼ tsp. cracked black pepper

1. Preheat the oven to 205°C. Slice the baguette into 0.5-cm-thick rounds.
2. Arrange the slices on a baking tray and place on the middle rack of the oven. Toast them for about 5 minutes, or until they become a bit hard and light brown on the edges.
3. Remove them from the oven, and let cool completely.
4. Meanwhile, drain the chopped tomatoes in a colander. In a large bowl, combine the tomatoes with the herbs, garlic, and onion. Then add the oil and the vinegar, salt, and pepper.
5. Refrigerate the mixture for at least 30 minutes so the flavours can meld. Top each toasted baguette slice with tomato mixture.

Nutrition Info per Serving:
Calories: 239, Protein: 6 g, Fat: 9 g, Carbohydrates: 32 g, Fibre: 3 g, Sugar: 5 g, Sodium: 386 mg

Grilled Aubergine and Courgette with Balsamic Vinegar

PREP TIME: 7 MINUTES, COOK TIME: 20 MINUTES, SERVES: 4

- 4 tbsps. extra virgin olive oil
- 1 large aubergine, sliced into 1-cm rounds
- 2 courgettes, sliced lengthwise
- 6 tbsps. balsamic vinegar
- ¼ tsp. sea salt, divided
- ⅛ tsp. cracked black pepper
- ¼ tsp. dried parsley
- ¼ tsp. dried basil
- ¼ tsp. dried oregano

1. Preheat grill to medium heat.
2. Lay the sliced aubergine on paper towels, and sprinkle each slice with a pinch of salt to pull out excess moisture. After 10 to 15 minutes, pat the slices dry with paper towels. Arrange the aubergine and courgettes on a baking tray with edges on it. Sprinkle pepper and dried herbs over the veggies, and drizzle with vinegar and oil.
3. Grill the veggies on a hot grill or grill pan for 4 to 6 minutes, flipping halfway through.
4. Remove from the grill or grill pan and serve.

Nutrition Info per Serving:
Calories: 196, Protein: 2 g, Fat: 15 g, Carbohydrates: 15 g, Fibre: 4 g, Sugar: 9 g, Sodium: 157 mg

Spicy Sun Dried Tomato Hummus

PREP TIME: 10 MINUTES, COOK TIME: 2 MINUTES, SERVES: 8

- 5 tbsps. extra virgin olive oil, divided
- 2 (425-g) cans chickpeas, rinsed and drained
- 60 ml tahini paste
- Juice of 2 lemons
- 2 large cloves garlic
- 2 tbsps. sun-roasted tomato slices
- 1 dried red chilli
- ½ tsp. sea salt
- ½ tsp. cracked black pepper

1. Place the chickpeas, tahini, lemon juice, garlic, tomato, chilli, salt, and pepper in a food processor. While processing, drizzle the oil until there are no large pieces and the hummus is smooth.
2. Add more water according to desired consistency and continue. 1 tbsp. water at a time, and taste and adjust.
3. Transfer to a serving dish, top with dried oregano and a drizzle of olive oil, and serve.

Nutrition Info per Serving:
Calories: 298, Protein: 10 g, Fat: 19 g, Carbohydrates: 26 g, Fibre: 7 g, Sugar: 4 g, Sodium: 231 mg

Chapter 13: Snack and Dessert

Cajun Courgette Chips

🕒 PREP TIME: 5 MINUTES, COOK TIME: 15 TO 16 MINUTES, SERVES: 4

- 2 large courgettes, cut into 3-mm-thick slices
- 2 tsps. Cajun seasoning
- Cooking spray

1. Preheat the air fryer to 190ºC.
2. Spray the air fryer basket lightly with cooking spray.
3. Put the courgette slices in a medium bowl and spray them generously with cooking spray.
4. Sprinkle the Cajun seasoning over the courgette and stir to make sure they are evenly coated with oil and seasoning.
5. Place the slices in a single layer in the air fryer basket, making sure not to overcrowd. You will need to cook these in several batches.
6. Air fry for 8 minutes. Flip the slices over and air fry for an additional 7 to 8 minutes, or until they are as crisp and brown as you prefer.
7. Serve immediately.

Nutrition Info per Serving:
Calories: 47, Protein: 2 g, Fat: 1 g, Carbohydrates: 9 g, Fibre: 3 g, Sugar: 4 g, Sodium: 319 mg

Carrot Cupcakes

🕒 PREP TIME: 10 MINUTES, COOK TIME: 35 MINUTES, SERVES: 12

- 240 g carrots, grated
- 240 g low fat cream cheese, soft
- 2 eggs
- 1-2 tsps. skim milk
- 125 ml coconut oil, melted
- 30 g coconut flour
- 50 g erythritol
- ¼ tsp. liquid stevia
- 2 tsps. vanilla, divided
- 1 tsp. baking powder
- 1 tsp. ground cinnamon
- Nonstick cooking spray

1. Heat oven to 180ºC. Lightly spray a muffin pan with cooking spray, or use paper liners.
2. In a large bowl, stir together the flour, baking powder, and cinnamon.
3. Add the carrots, eggs, oil, erythritol, and vanilla to a food processor. Process until ingredients are combined but carrots still have some large chunks remaining. Add to dry ingredients and stir to combine.
4. Pour evenly into prepared pan, filling cups ⅔ full. Bake for 30-35 minutes, or until cupcakes pass the toothpick test. Remove from oven and let cool.
5. In a medium bowl, beat cream cheese, stevia, and vanilla on high speed until smooth. Add milk, one tsp. at a time, beating after each addition, until frosting is creamy enough to spread easily.
6. Once cupcakes have cooled, spread each one with about 2 tbsps. of frosting. Chill until ready to serve.

Nutrition Info per Serving:
Calories: 223, Protein: 4 g, Fat: 18 g, Carbohydrates: 12 g, Fibre: 3 g, Sugar: 4 g, Sodium: 148 mg

Rosemary Baked Cashews

🕒 PREP TIME: 5 MINUTES, COOK TIME: 3 MINUTES, SERVES: 4

- 2 sprigs of fresh rosemary (1 chopped and 1 whole)
- 1 tsp. olive oil
- 1 tsp. coarse salt
- 1 drop liquid stevia
- 300 g roasted and unsalted whole cashews
- Cooking spray

1. Preheat the air fryer to 150ºC.
2. In a medium bowl, whisk together the chopped rosemary, olive oil, coarse salt, and stevia. Set aside.
3. Spray the air fryer basket with cooking spray, then place the cashews and the whole rosemary sprig in the basket and bake for 3 minutes.
4. Remove the cashews and rosemary from the air fryer, then discard the rosemary and add the cashews to the olive oil mixture, tossing to coat.
5. Allow to cool for 15 minutes before serving.

Nutrition Info per Serving:
Calories: 255, Protein: 8 g, Fat: 21 g, Carbohydrates: 11 g, Fibre: 2 g, Sugar: 1 g, Sodium: 584 mg

Spicy Kale Chips

🕒 PREP TIME: 5 MINUTES, COOK TIME: 8 TO 12 MINUTES, SERVES: 4

- 180 g kale, large stems removed and chopped
- 2 tsps. rapeseed oil
- ¼ tsp. smoked paprika
- ¼ tsp. coarse salt
- Cooking spray

1. Preheat the air fryer to 200ºC.
2. In a large bowl, toss the kale, rapeseed oil, smoked paprika, and coarse salt.
3. Spray the air fryer basket with cooking spray, then place half the kale in the basket and air fry for 2 to 3 minutes.
4. Shake the basket and air fry for 2 to 3 more minutes, or until crispy. Repeat this process with the remaining kale.
5. Remove the kale and allow to cool on a wire rack for 3 to 5 minutes before serving.

Nutrition Info per Serving:
Calories: 57, Protein: 2 g, Fat: 3 g, Carbohydrates: 7 g, Fibre: 2 g, Sugar: 0 g, Sodium: 210 mg

Cream Cheese Pound Cake

⏱ PREP TIME: 10 MINUTES, COOK TIME: 35 MINUTES, SERVES: 14

- 4 eggs
- 100 g fat free cream cheese, soft
- 4 tbsps. almond butter, soft
- 125 g ground almonds
- 140 g erythritol
- 1 tsp. baking powder
- 1 tsp. vanilla
- ¼ tsp. salt
- Butter flavoured cooking spray

1. Heat oven to 180ºC. Spray an 20-cm loaf pan with cooking spray.
2. In a medium bowl, combine ground almonds, baking powder, and salt.
3. In a large bowl, beat almond butter and erythritol until light and fluffy. Add cream cheese and vanilla and beat well.
4. Add the eggs, one at a time, beating after each one. Stir in the dry ingredients until thoroughly combined.
5. Pour into prepared pan and bake for 30-40 minutes or cake passes the toothpick test. Let cool 10 minutes in the pan, then invert onto serving plate. Slice and serve.

Nutrition Info per Serving:
Calories: 165, Protein: 6 g, Fat: 13 g, Carbohydrates: 6 g, Fibre: 2 g, Sugar: 1 g, Sodium: 90 mg

Spicy Chicken Bites

⏱ PREP TIME: 10 MINUTES, COOK TIME: 10 TO 12 MINUTES, MAKES: 30 BITES

- 250 g boneless and skinless chicken thighs, cut into 30 pieces
- ¼ tsp. coarse salt
- 2 tbsps. hot sauce
- Cooking spray

1. Preheat the air fryer to 200ºC.
2. Spray the air fryer basket with cooking spray and season the chicken bites with the coarse salt, then place in the basket and air fry for 10 to 12 minutes or until crispy.
3. While the chicken bites cook, pour the hot sauce into a large bowl.
4. Remove the bites and add to the sauce bowl, tossing to coat. Serve warm.

Nutrition Info per Serving:
Calories: 16, Protein: 2 g, Fat: 1 g, Carbohydrates: 0 g, Fibre: 0 g, Sugar: 0 g, Sodium: 60 mg

Herbed Pitta Chips

PREP TIME: 5 MINUTES, COOK TIME: 5 TO 6 MINUTES, SERVES: 4

- ¼ tsp. dried basil
- ¼ tsp. marjoram
- ¼ tsp. ground oregano
- ¼ tsp. garlic powder
- ¼ tsp. ground thyme
- ¼ tsp. salt
- 2 (15-cm) wholemeal pittas
- Cooking spray

1. Preheat the air fryer to 165°C.
2. Mix all the seasonings together.
3. Cut each pitta half into 4 wedges. Break apart wedges at the fold.
4. Mist one side of pitta wedges with oil. Sprinkle with half of seasoning mix.
5. Turn pitta wedges over, mist the other side with oil, and sprinkle with remaining seasonings.
6. Place pitta wedges in air fryer basket and bake for 2 minutes.
7. Shake the basket and bake for 2 minutes longer. Shake again, and if needed, bake for 1 or 2 more minutes, or until crisp. Watch carefully because at this point they will cook very quickly.
8. Serve hot.

Nutrition Info per Serving:
Calories: 80, Protein: 2 g, Fat: 1 g, Carbohydrates: 16 g, Fibre: 2 g, Sugar: 0 g, Sodium: 199 mg

....

Cauliflower Tots

PREP TIME: 15 MINUTES, COOK TIME: 23 MINUTES, SERVES: 6

- 250 ml water
- 1 head cauliflower, broken into florets
- 2 eggs, beaten
- 50 g grated low-fat Parmesan cheese
- 50 g grated low-fat Emmental cheese
- 2 tbsps. fresh coriander, chopped
- 1 shallot, chopped
- Sea salt and ground black pepper, to taste

1. Add the water to the Instant Pot. Set a steamer basket in the pot.
2. Arrange the cauliflower florets in the steamer basket.
3. Secure the lid. Choose the Manual mode and set the cooking time for 3 minutes at High Pressure.
4. Once cooking is complete, perform a quick pressure release. Carefully open the lid.
5. Mash the cauliflower in a food processor and add the remaining ingredients. Pulse to combine well.
6. Form the mixture into a tater-tot shape with oiled hands.
7. Place cauliflower tots on a lightly greased baking sheet. Bake in the preheated oven at 205°C for about 20 minutes. Flip halfway through the cooking time.
8. Serve immediately.

Nutrition Info per Serving:
Calories: 85, Protein: 7 g, Fat: 3 g, Carbohydrates: 9 g, Fibre: 4 g, Sugar: 3 g, Sodium: 207 mg

Blackberry Crostata

PREP TIME: 10 MINUTES, COOK TIME: 20 MINUTES, SERVES: 6

- 1 (22-cm) wholemeal pie crust, unbaked
- 240 g fresh blackberries
- Juice and zest of 1 lemon
- 2 tbsps. almond butter, soft
- 3 tbsps. erythritol, divided
- 2 tbsps. cornflour

1. Heat oven to 220°C. Line a large baking sheet with parchment paper and unroll pie crust in pan.
2. In a medium bowl, combine blackberries, 2 tbsps. erythritol, lemon juice and zest, and cornflour. Spoon onto crust leaving a 5-cm edge. Fold and crimp the edges.
3. Dot the berries with 1 tbsp. almond butter. Brush the crust edge with remaining butter and sprinkle crust and fruit with remaining erythritol.
4. Bake for 20-22 minutes or until golden brown. Cool before cutting and serving.

Nutrition Info per Serving:
Calories: 250, Protein: 4 g, Fat: 15 g, Carbohydrates: 27 g, Fibre: 4 g, Sugar: 3 g, Sodium: 160 mg

Cinnamon Bread Pudding

PREP TIME: 10 MINUTES, COOK TIME: 45 MINUTES, SERVES: 6

- 250 g day-old French or Italian bread, cut into 2-cm cubes
- 500 ml skim milk
- 2 egg whites
- 1 egg
- 4 tbsps. almond butter, sliced
- 5 tsps. erythritol
- 1½ tsps. cinnamon
- ¼ tsp. salt
- ⅛ tsp. ground cloves

1. Heat oven to 180°C.
2. In a medium sauce pan, heat milk and almond butter to simmering. Remove from heat and stir until almond butter is completely melted. Let cool 10 minutes.
3. In a large bowl, beat egg and egg whites until foamy. Add erythritol, spices and salt. Beat until combined, then add in cooled milk and bread.
4. Transfer mixture to a 1.5-litre baking dish. Place on rack of roasting pan and add 2.5-cm of hot water to roaster.
5. Bake until pudding is set and knife inserted in centre comes out clean, about 40-45 minutes.

Nutrition Info per Serving:
Calories: 275, Protein: 10 g, Fat: 10 g, Carbohydrates: 35 g, Fibre: 3 g, Sugar: 3 g, Sodium: 353 mg

Appendix 1: Measurement Conversion Chart

WEIGHT EQUIVALENTS

METRIC	US STANDARD	US STANDARD (OUNCES)
15 g	1 tablespoon	1/2 ounce
30 g	1/8 cup	1 ounce
60 g	1/4 cup	2 ounces
115 g	1/2 cup	4 ounces
170 g	3/4 cup	6 ounces
225 g	1 cup	8 ounces
450 g	2 cups	16 ounces
900 g	4 cups	2 pounds

VOLUME EQUIVALENTS

METRIC	US STANDARD	US STANDARD (OUNCES)
15 ml	1 tablespoon	1/2 fl.oz.
30 ml	2 tablespoons	1 fl.oz.
60 ml	1/4 cup	2 fl.oz.
125 ml	1/2 cup	4 fl.oz.
180 ml	3/4 cup	6 fl.oz.
250 ml	1 cup	8 fl.oz.
500 ml	2 cups	16 fl.oz.
1000 ml	4 cups	1 quart

TEMPERATURES EQUIVALENTS

CELSIUS (C)	FAHRENHEIT (F) (APPROXIMATE)
120 °C	250 °F
135 °C	275 °F
150 °C	300 °F
160 °C	325 °F
175 °C	350 °F
190 °C	375 °F
205 °C	400 °F
220 °C	425 °F
230 °C	450 °F
245°C	475 °F
260 °C	500 °F

LENGTH EQUIVALENTS

METRIC	IMPERIAL
3 mm	1/8 inch
6 mm	1/4 inch
1 cm	1/2 inch
2.5 cm	1 inch
3 cm	1 1/4 inches
5 cm	2 inches
10 cm	4 inches
15 cm	6 inches
20 cm	8 inches

Appendix 2: 4-Week Meal Plan

Week-1	Breakfast	Lunch	Dinner	Snack/Dessert
Day-1	Homemade Cinnamon Rolls	Spicy Prawns	Grilled Ultimate Portobello Burger	Spicy Kale Chips
Day-2	Cheese Spinach Omelette	Easy Asian Turkey Meatballs	Adzuki Bean and Celery Soup	Cajun Courgette Chips
Day-3	Protein Spinach Waffles	Mushroom Spelt Bowl	Crock Pot Carnitas	Cream Cheese Pound Cake
Day-4	Spicy Shakshuka	Asian Fried Aubergine	Chicken Fajita Bowls	Cauliflower Tots
Day-5	Coconut Quinoa Breakfast Porridge	Classic Carrot Apple Salad	Turkey Spaghetti	Carrot Cupcakes
Day-6	French Asparagus and Courgette Omelette	Basil Tomato Pasta	Crumbed Golden Fillet Steak	Cinnamon Bread Pudding
Day-7	Baked Eggs with Zoodles	Slow Cooked Lamb Shanks	Breaded Flounder	Spicy Chicken Bites

Week-2	Breakfast	Lunch	Dinner	Snack/Dessert
Day-1	Apples and Walnuts Porridge	Cajun Smothered Pork Chops	Adzuki Bean and Celery Soup	Herbed Pitta Chips
Day-2	Egg and Mushroom Wild Rice Casserole	Cherry Tomato Farfalle with Pesto	Crumbed Golden Fillet Steak	Rosemary Baked Cashews
Day-3	Homemade Cinnamon Rolls	Classic Carrot Apple Salad	Sesame Seeds Coated Haddock	Spicy Kale Chips
Day-4	Cheese Spinach Omelette	Barbecue Chicken Wings	Quinoa with Spinach	Blackberry Crostata
Day-5	Spicy Shakshuka	Cod with Asparagus	Grilled Ultimate Portobello Burger	Cajun Courgette Chips
Day-6	Protein Spinach Waffles	Turkey Spaghetti	Slow Cooked Lamb Shanks	Spicy Chicken Bites
Day-7	Coconut Quinoa Breakfast Porridge	Chicken and Spinach Stew	Asian Fried Aubergine	Carrot Cupcakes

Week-3	Breakfast	Lunch	Dinner	Snack/Dessert
Day-1	Baked Eggs with Zoodles	Vegetarian Caramelised Onions	Chicken Fajita Bowls	Rosemary Baked Cashews
Day-2	French Asparagus and Courgette Omelette	Garlicky Lamb Chops	Basil Tomato Pasta	Cream Cheese Pound Cake
Day-3	Egg and Mushroom Wild Rice Casserole	Chicken Fettuccine Alfredo	Calamari Stew	Herbed Pitta Chips
Day-4	Savoury Turkey Patties	Breaded Flounder	Perfect Roasted Brussels Sprouts	Cajun Courgette Chips
Day-5	Homemade Cinnamon Rolls	Easy Asian Turkey Meatballs	Mushroom Spelt Bowl	Cinnamon Bread Pudding
Day-6	Apples and Walnuts Porridge	Chickpeas Curry	Crock Pot Carnitas	Spicy Kale Chips
Day-7	Cheese Spinach Omelette	Asparagus Salad	Spicy Prawns	Cauliflower Tots

Week-4	Breakfast	Lunch	Dinner	Snack/Dessert
Day-1	Spicy Shakshuka	Cod with Asparagus	Crock Pot Carnitas	Cream Cheese Pound Cake
Day-2	Coconut Quinoa Breakfast Porridge	Barbecue Chicken Wings	Cherry Tomato Farfalle with Pesto	Herbed Pitta Chips
Day-3	Protein Spinach Waffles	Quinoa with Spinach	Garlicky Lamb Chops	Rosemary Baked Cashews
Day-4	Apples and Walnuts Porridge	Spicy Prawns	Perfect Roasted Brussels Sprouts	Blackberry Crostata
Day-5	Baked Eggs with Zoodles	Chicken and Spinach Stew	Chickpeas Curry	Carrot Cupcakes
Day-6	Savoury Turkey Patties	Sesame Seeds Coated Haddock	Vegetarian Caramelised Onions	Spicy Chicken Bites
Day-7	French Asparagus and Courgette Omelette	Asparagus Salad	Chicken Fettuccine Alfredo	Cauliflower Tots

Appendix 3: Recipes Index

A

adzuki bean
Adzuki Bean and Celery Soup / 27
almond
Cream Cheese Pound Cake / 63
apple
Apples and Walnuts Porridge / 11
Apple and Pecan Quinoa Salad / 16
Classic Carrot Apple Salad / 48
artichoke
Breaded Artichoke Hearts / 34
Artichoke-Spinach Dip / 56
asparagus
French Asparagus and Courgette Omelette / 9
Asparagus Salad / 50
Healthy Grilled Asparagus / 58
aubergine
Asian Fried Aubergine / 35
avocado
Avocado Cucumber Feta Salad / 47
Cherry Tomato and Avocado Salad / 50

B

beef
Minced Beef Pasta / 19
beef braising steak
Braising Steak with Brussels Sprouts / 42
beef sirloin
Spinach and Beef Stew / 52
beetroot
Roasted Beetroot and Pistachio Salad / 50
Delicious Roasted Beetroot Soup / 53
Black Bean
Herbed Black Beans / 23
Black Bean and Tomato Soup with Lime Yoghurt / 26
Easy Three-Bean Medley / 26
Blackberry
Blackberry Crostata / 65
black-eyed bean
Black-Eyed Beans with Collard / 27
blueberry
Coconut Quinoa Breakfast Porridge / 13
Blueberry Wild Rice / 17
Brussels sprouts
Perfect Roasted Brussels Sprouts / 32

C

calamari
Calamari Stew / 51
cannellini bean
Rosemary White Beans with Onion / 24
Carrot and Bean Chilli / 51
carrot
Carrot Cupcakes / 61
cashew
Rosemary Baked Cashews / 62
cauliflower
Low-Carb Cauliflower Mash / 33
Roasted Cauliflower with Lemon Zest / 34
Cauliflower Mushroom Risotto / 36
Creamy Vegetable Soup / 54
Cauliflower Tots / 64
Cherry
Spelt and Cherry Salad / 17
cherry tomato
Cherry Tomato Farfalle with Pesto / 20
Caprese Salad Quinoa Bowl / 48
chicken
Chicken Fettuccine Alfredo / 18
chicken breast
Mexican Black Bean and Chicken Soup / 25
Chicken and Spinach Stew / 37
Chicken and Mushroom Casserole / 38
Chicken Fajita Bowls / 40
Broccoli Chicken with Black Beans / 40
Chicken Curry / 41
Tomato Chicken Soup / 54
chicken thigh
Spicy Chicken Bites / 63
chicken wing
Barbecue Chicken Wings / 37
chickpea
Chickpeas Curry / 23
Chickpea Salad with Olives and Cucumber / 49
Spicy Sun Dried Tomato Hummus / 60
cod
Cod with Asparagus / 28
Chinese Style Cod / 29
Cod Cakes / 30
courgette
Baked Eggs with Zoodles / 12
Sesame Noodle and Courgette Bowl / 22
Grilled Aubergine and Courgette with Balsamic Vinegar / 60
Cajun Courgette Chips / 61

E-H

English cucumber
Tzatziki Greek Yoghurt Dip / 57
fig
Nut Buckwheat Pilaf / 16

fillet steak
Crumbed Golden Fillet Steak / 45
flounder
Breaded Flounder / 31
green cabbage
Sautéed Cabbage / 32
green lentil
Green Lentil and Carrot Stew / 24
green olive
Air Fried Olives / 58
haddock
Sesame Seeds Coated Haddock / 31
halibut
Thyme-Sesame Crusted Halibut / 31
heirloom tomato
Classic Bruschetta / 59

J-M,O
Japanese aubergine
Baba Ghanoush / 57
Kalamata olive
Caper and Olive Pasta / 19
kale
Spicy Kale Chips / 62
lamb chop
Garlicky Lamb Chops / 43
lamb rack
Lamb Rack with Pesto Sauce / 43
Nut Crusted Rack of Lamb / 46
lamb shank
Slow Cooked Lamb Shanks / 44
mushroom
Egg and Mushroom Wild Rice Casserole / 13
Mushroom Spelt Bowl / 15
Spinach and Mushroom Pasta / 20
onion
Wild Rice with Parsley / 14

P
pea
Mint and Pea Risotto / 14
pecan
Couscous with Balsamic Dressing / 15
pepper
Spicy Shakshuka / 11
plum tomato
Ratatouille with Herbs / 35
pork butt
Crock Pot Carnitas / 45
pork chop
Cajun Smothered Pork Chops / 46
pork loin chop
Garlic Pork Chops / 44

portobello mushroom
Grilled Ultimate Portobello Burger / 36
prawn
Spicy Prawns / 28
Simple Grilled Prawn / 59

R
red lentil
Quick Lentil Bisque / 55
red pepper
Pearl Barley with Peppers / 17
Red Peppers and Anchovy Antipasto / 56
ribeye steak
Air Fried Ribeye Steak / 42

S
salmon
Thai Fish Curry / 29
Simple Salmon / 30
Spanish onion
Basil Tomato Pasta / 21
spinach
Protein Spinach Waffles / 9
Cheese Spinach Omelette / 12
Quinoa with Spinach / 17
Creamy Tomato Pasta with Spinach / 21
stewing beef
Beef Tomato Stew / 53
Mushroom and Beef Chilli / 55

T
tomato
Penne Pasta with Tomato-Vodka Sauce / 22
Lentils with Spinach / 25
Quick Chopped Caprese Salad / 47
Tomato and Bean Stew / 52
tuna
Tuna Salad with Lettuce / 31
Lemon Avocado Tuna Salad / 49
turkey
Turkey Spaghetti / 18
Turkey Hoisin Burgers / 39
Easy Asian Turkey Meatballs / 41
turkey breast
Savoury Turkey Patties / 13
Herbed Turkey Breast / 38

W
white kidney bean
Tuscan Tuna and Bean Salad / 50
white onion
Vegetarian Caramelised Onions / 33
Whole Chicken
Whole Chicken Roast / 39

Printed in Great Britain
by Amazon